"Classic Andy—accessible to any of us wanting to change, yet deep enough to challenge you if you think you know the answers."

—MAX LUCADO, pastor and *New York Times* bestselling author

"It seems the more important the decision, the more we struggle making it. In this much needed message, Andy provides us with the wisdom we need and the questions we can ask that will lead us to choices that can improve our lives. I don't know about you, but my life is complicated enough without the confusion of uncertainty or, even worse, the turmoil of regret. This book is not just a necessary guide to better decisions—it's a handbook for life that is sure to make a difference in yours."

—LYSA TERKEURST, #1 *New York Times* bestselling author and president of Proverbs 31 Ministries

"Andy is a voice I've trusted in my life for a long time. One of the dozen things I like about Andy is that he doesn't varnish the truth but will tell us the way it is with kindness and a boatload of wisdom. This is the right book for the right time. We've got some important decisions to make and this book will help frame the right questions to ask."

—BOB GOFF, Sweet Maria's husband and *New York Times* bestselling author of *Love Does*, *Everybody Always*, and *Dream Big*

"When we were kids, we were warned about making faces because they might get stuck that way. In *Better Decisions, Fewer Regrets*, Andy Stanley helps us see a caution light that extends far beyond sticking out your tongue and crinkling up your forehead. In these pages you will discover that time doesn't change anything—it just makes you more of what you are today. Future you is an exaggerated version of current you. In the end, the life you get 'stuck' with is the life you make. Now is the time to change your choices to regret-proof your future. Andy will show you how."

—**LEVI LUSKO,** pastor of Fresh
Life Church and author

"Andy Stanley strikes again! This challenging, practical, and engaging book will help you make better decisions and lead to the life you really want. If you're looking for a book that's brimming with wisdom, insightful teaching, and that signature Andy Stanley humor, then look no further—this is it! I can't recommend it highly enough!"

—**IAN MORGAN CRON,** author,
The Road Back to You

Wow, in this book Andy uses insights, understanding, and even humor to bring great clarity to the life-altering decisions we will all have to make. Deciding to get this book now could absolutely lead to fewer regrets later.

—**MICHAEL JR.**

better
decisions,
fewer
regrets

better decisions, fewer regrets

— 5 —
QUESTIONS
TO HELP DETERMINE
YOUR NEXT MOVE

ANDY STANLEY

ZONDERVAN
REFLECTIVE

ZONDERVAN

Better Decisions, Fewer Regrets
Copyright © 2020 by Andy Stanley

Requests for information should be addressed to:
Zondervan, *3900 Sparks Dr. SE, Grand Rapids, Michigan 49546*

Zondervan titles may be purchased in bulk for educational, business, fundraising, or sales promotional use. For information, please email SpecialMarkets@Zondervan.com.

ISBN 978-0-310-53708-3 (hardcover)

ISBN 978-0-310-53713-7 (audio)

ISBN 978-0-310-53710-6 (ebook)

Library of Congress Cataloging-in-Publication Data

Cover Design: Brand Navigation
Cover Image: © *Luhuangfeng / iStockphoto*
Interior Design: Kait Lamphere

Printed in the United States of America

22 23 24 25 26 27 /LSC/ 13 12 11 10 9 8 7

For Andrew, Garrett, and Allie
Couldn't be prouder of the paths you've
chosen and the stories you're writing.

—DAD

Contents

Introduction

My dad had a terrible habit.

I thought it was terrible, anyway.

He wouldn't tell me what to do.

Specifically, he wouldn't tell me what to do when I didn't know what to do and *wanted* him to tell me what *he thought* I should do.

True, most kids don't want their parents telling them what to do. And I was like most kids most of the time. But on occasion, I wanted him to tell me what to do. And he wouldn't. Worse, instead of answering my questions, he asked me questions! His go-to question was: What are you going to do when I'm not around to tell you what to do?

My go-to response was: But you *are* around, so tell me!

Clearly, his response did not indicate a lack of interest on his part. Just the opposite. As it turns out, I employed the same strategy with my kids . . . or tried to anyway. Maybe one day they'll write a book about it.

His go-to question wasn't his only question. During middle school and high school, his arsenal of questions included one of the five we will explore later: *What is the wise thing to do?* As a teenager, that pesky question usually eliminated most of my preferred options. But when I leaned in, it eliminated unnecessary regret as well.

What I didn't appreciate then, that I most certainly appreciate now, was *why*. Why all the questions? Why not just tell me what he thought I should do? The reason was simple. He was teaching me how to make decisions. Good decisions. He started early. Maybe too early. But to his credit and my advantage, he started when the stakes were low.

Perhaps unbeknownst to him, my dad was teaching me something else as well. That something else is the point of this little book. By opting for questions over direction, my dad connected two important dots for me. Dots many folks never connect. He helped me make the connection between *good* questions and *good* decisions. To tease that out a bit, he helped me make the connection between *well*-placed, *appropriately* timed, *thought*-provoking questions and good decision-making. Simply put:

Good *questions* lead to better *decisions*.

And better decisions lead to fewer regrets.

This is why, on the back side of a bad decision, it's not unusual to hear someone say, "I should have asked more questions." Why? Because we know intuitively that the more questions we ask, the more information we acquire, which leads to greater insight and, hopefully, better decisions. But pausing to ponder a list of potentially disruptive questions is neither easy nor intuitive.

Truth is, most of us *resist* uninvited questions when making a decision. In the moment, we feel like we're being *questioned* rather than simply being asked a *question*. Big difference. When we confuse one for the other, our defenses go up and our learning aptitude goes down. It's virtually impossible to welcome new information or insight when we're convinced our judgment is being questioned. This is especially true when making personal decisions. After all, they're personal! Translated, it's nobody's business.

But let's be honest.

You've never made a *personal* decision that didn't become somebody's business. Private decisions almost always have *public* ramifications. Right? Every decision we make impacts somebody in our public, beginning with the folks closest to us. There's no getting around the fact that *well*-placed, *appropriately* timed, *thought*-provoking questions result in better decisions and fewer regrets.

Clay Christensen, a professor at Harvard Business School, said, "Questions are places in your mind where answers fit. If you haven't asked the question, the answer has nowhere to go. It hits your mind and bounces right off. You have to ask the question—you have to want to know—in order to open up the space for the answer to fit."

BREADCRUMBS

Good counselors understand this. Counselors understand that we hominids have a greater propensity to follow through on decisions *we make* rather than advice *prescribed* to us. So counselors painstakingly scatter breadcrumbs along our paths to lead us toward making our own good decisions. The breadcrumbs are . . . you guessed it . . . *well*-placed, *appropriately* timed, *thought*-provoking questions.

But . . .

But what if you knew the questions ahead of time?

What if you had a list of questions you could *ask your-self* when faced with important decisions? Imagine the money you would save by avoiding all those trips to the counselor!

Kidding.

Sort of.

Seriously, imagine having a list of questions that served as the grid or filter by which to evaluate your options? If the idea of a decision-making grid strikes you as odd, it shouldn't. You already have one. You use it every day. You just aren't aware of it. Every time you make a decision, you unconsciously ask questions such as:

- Will this make me happy?
- Will I enjoy this?
- Will this hurt me?
- Will this hurt anybody else?
- Will anyone find out?

While some questions we intuitively ask ourselves are helpful, others aren't, especially those first two. Those first two are essential ingredients in the recipe for regret.

Familiar with that recipe?

Yeah. We all are.

My purpose in writing this book is to give you the questions ahead of time. Not *all* the questions. But five questions I'm convinced will result in better decisions and fewer regrets.

I want to add *five questions* to your existing arsenal of questions. Five questions to ask every time you make a decision of any consequence. These questions are so simple that once you see the list, you may wonder if you even need to finish the book.

That's up to you.

But before you go looking for your receipt, consider this:

> There is no necessary correlation
> between *knowing* and *doing*.

There should be. But there isn't. Knowing the questions to ask and actually pausing to ask them are two completely different things. And although we've never met, I can promise you this. Developing the discipline to pause and ask these five questions *will* result in *better decisions* and *fewer regrets*. So I hope you'll finish the book. My hope is that these five questions will inform your conscience and in that way become permanent fixtures in your decision-making process.

Here they are:

The Integrity Question: Am I being honest with
    myself . . . really?
The Legacy Question: What story do I want to tell?
The Conscience Question: Is there a tension that
    deserves my attention?
The Maturity Question: What is the wise thing to do?
The Relationship Question: What does love require
    of me?

In chapters two through six, we will take a deep dive
and unpack each of the five questions. But first, I need to
highlight one extraordinarily important, but easy-to-miss
relationship between your *decisions* and your *future*.

— 1 —

More Than a Decision

Life is all about decision-making. Every day. Multiple times a day. Sometimes we're sure. Sometime we're unsure. Some of us are quick to decide. Others of us (me included) can't ever get enough information before we decide. But in the end, we are where we are because of decisions we've made. Our futures will be determined by our decisions as well.

Your decisions . . . along with your responses to other people's decisions, which are also your decisions . . . are about the only thing you can control in life, which means your decisions are *how* you control your life. Decisions are your steering wheel. Your joystick. Your keypad. Which means . . . and this is big: Your decisions determine your story.

The story of your life.

Every decision becomes a permanent part of our stories. That being the case, we should stop at every decision-making juncture and consider *the story we want to tell.* Perhaps more compelling, we should consider what story we want told about us. The good news is that you get to decide. But you decide one decision at a time because you write the story of your life . . . one decision at a time.

Our decisions determine the direction and quality of our lives. Your decisions have shaped the direction and quality of your life so far—for good and for . . . well, maybe not so good. You are where you are for the most part because of decisions *you've* made.

So yeah, it's your fault.

I thought we should get that out of the way up front.

But it's not all bad news.

Regret and disappointment aren't the only things spilling out of your decision pipeline. Your greatest joys and accomplishments are as well. Moral of the story: regardless of how things are going or have gone, *you* are responsible for *you*. You get to write the story.

If you're like most people, you would like to go back and unmake a few decisions—the decisions that led to the chapters of your life you wish you could go back and unlive. Or relive. Perhaps you emerged from that not-so-glorious season of life committed to making better decisions in the future. Perhaps you have. Oddly enough, most people don't.

Most people don't learn from bad decisions because they're convinced their bad decisions were somebody else's fault. So, as long as they stay away from "somebody else," no real change is required on their end. You've seen that. It's easy to see when it's somebody else. It's practically impossible to see it in the mirror.

More on that later as well.

If you think back to the last decision you'd like to unmake, you won't have to think back too far. The breakfast you skipped. The lunch you ate. The CrossFit class you didn't attend. Again. The bed you left unmade . . . that leaves someone else feeling like your maid. Low-impact decisions for sure, but decisions you participated in. In fact, you were there for all your bad decisions . . . and the good ones as well. But you're not reading a book about decision-making because you've conquered the beast. So . . . back to your latest not-so-great decision.

Just stop.

Stop making bad decisions. *Bad* decisions don't result in a *good* life. Bad relationship decisions don't result in good relationships. Bad financial decisions don't result in . . . you know this.

So stop. And return this book before you're tempted to underline something.

If only it were that easy, right? If it were that easy, there wouldn't be such a long line at Jeni's. You've had Jeni's ice cream, right? If not . . . well . . . I'm sorry I brought it up.

Some of our bad decisions simply embarrass us. Others set us back. Some scar us. Others cripple us. Making four payments of $29.95 for something that's only worth $29.95 is embarrassing. But $25,000 in consumer debt can be crippling. Picking a stock that was supposed to double in value . . . but didn't . . . is eventually nothing more than an embarrassing story you tell. Picking a marriage partner in spite of multiple red flags and dozens of phone calls from your momma . . . something else entirely.

IT'S COMPLICATED

One reason we don't learn from experience, in spite of our intelligence, is that decision-making is heavily influenced by something more than past experiences or even the past experiences of others. Our decisions are heavily influenced by our emotions and our appetites. Research suggests we aren't able to make decisions *apart* from our emotions. Experience confirms our appetites often overrule our intelligence. Otherwise nobody would have to remind us to exercise and eat right.

Decisions are never made in an emotionally neutral environment. When it comes to decisions pertaining to you, there are no emotionally neutral environments. This is why it's often easier for you to know what your neighbor, spouse, or partner at work should do than what you should do. This is why we say things like, "Easy for me to say." Or when talking to our kids, "Do as I say, not as I do." Which never works.

Both statements are admissions that we *know* better than we *do*, which flies in the face of both intelligence and experience. But again, our decisions are governed by forces stronger than either. Knowing the intelligent thing to do in no way ensures we do what's intelligent. Knowing the right thing to do doesn't guarantee anything.

So what should we do?

We should put ourselves in time-out.

We should pause and ask *five questions*.

But enough about us for a moment. Let's shift the spotlight to those "other people."

POOR PLANNING

When we see other people make what we know to be bad decisions, it's as if they are strategically and intentionally undermining their own happiness. It takes a lot of planning to marry someone you are incompatible with. It takes time and energy to launch a business built on faulty assumptions and poor market analysis. Think about all the paperwork couples have to wade through to purchase a house they can't afford or apply for a loan they will struggle to repay. In most cases, these weren't spur-of-the-moment decisions. It took planning.

They planned a regret.

Ever planned a regret?

That's regrettable.

Sorry.

Nobody decides to blow up a marriage. But every divorce is on the tail end of a string of decisions, including the decision to get married in the first place. Nobody decides to raise irresponsible, codependent children. But like you, I've watched parents make decisions that aimed their children in that direction. Nobody decides to be addicted. But every addiction is connected to decisions. Nobody plans to bury themselves under a mountain of credit card debt. But the people who find themselves buried there buried themselves one purchasing decision at a time.

Nobody *plans* to complicate their life with a bad decision. The problem is . . . what moved me to write this book is . . . too many people *don't plan not to*. They don't *plan* not to complicate their lives with unnecessary, completely avoidable bad decisions. They don't put simple safeguards in place to ensure a more-happily-ever-after ending.

These five questions are a safeguard.

SELLING IT

You may not be good at selling anything to anybody else, but when it comes to selling yourself on a bad idea, you are master class. Right? Me too. Our greatest regrets are associated with things, "opportunities," and people we sold ourselves on.

Think back to your last bad relationship decision. Seemed right at the time. You were in love. Or lust. Or something. Whatever it was, you were in it. And whereas it may not have been rational, it was certainly emotional. Of course it was. Relationships are emotional. Your momma tried to warn you. Your best friend tried to warn you. But you assured them you knew what you were doing, and at the time you *were* sure you knew what you were doing. But looking back, you wonder, *What was I doing? I should have known better. I should have listened. I should have seen that freight train coming.*

How 'bout this . . .

Your most recent bad purchasing decision.

Perhaps this book.

Hope not.

We've all made bad purchasing decisions. But once you had your heart set on *it*, whatever *it* was, it was over. It was like something took over, and the next thing you knew you were handing your credit card to someone you didn't know to buy something you didn't need and perhaps couldn't or shouldn't afford.

So much for intellect and experience. Something else took over.

That something else was—you. You took over. You started selling yourself. As it turns out, you are a sucker for you! We will explore this odd dynamic in more depth later, but in case later never comes, I'll go ahead and tease you with a tip: As soon as *you* start selling *you* on anything, *you* should hit pause. Here's why. We rarely have to sell ourselves on a good idea.

Again.

We rarely have to sell ourselves on a *good* idea.

We just know, don't we?

Later I'll tell you how to stop selling and start listening.

SURPRISE!

The most difficult decision-making environments are the ones we didn't anticipate, the ones that take us by surprise. Purchasing decisions, choosing a school, selecting a vacation destination, or navigating a menu at a new restaurant, we see those decisions coming. But along the way, we are all forced to make decisions we never imagined we'd have to make. Surprise decisions.

A job offer comes along and you have one week to decide.

Surprise.

You're already in a relationship and then someone you never expected to show interest in you starts showing interest.

Surprise.

Or maybe you're in a relationship . . . and you thought things were going well, and then you discover disturbing information about Mr. or Ms. Right. Now, you have to decide whether to rock the boat or look the other way.

Surprise.

Surprise decisions. Don't you hate 'em? If you're a parent, surprise decisions are a way of life. At some point along the way, you might have even said, "I wish I didn't have to decide," or "I wish somebody would decide for me."

The challenging thing about surprise decisions is the time frame. It's usually short. Because the time frame is compressed, we rarely have time to get the information we need to make a good decision. But the decision must be made!

If you've ever found yourself in a toxic relationship, you know what I'm talking about. By toxic, I mean the relationship wasn't good for you. The other person wasn't necessarily bad. But they were bad for you. You were bad together. Things started out fine, but over time, well, it got unhealthy. Toxic. Like most folks in toxic relationships, you downplayed the bad and focused on the good. After all, you liked him. But you were becoming more like him. And you didn't necessarily like what you were becoming.

Then somebody pointed it out.

You had a decision to make.

A decision you never thought you'd have to make. A decision you didn't want to make. A decision you were trying to avoid. Either way you decided, you would lose something. You would lose a friend or you would continue to lose you. You couldn't have it both ways. You may be in a situation like that right now. It may be why somebody gave you this book. It's a terrible place to be.

Good luck.

Actually, keep reading.

And then there's this—the perspective most folks consider *last* when, in fact, they should consider it *first*.

YOUR FINGERPRINTS ON THE FUTURE

Legacy is a term that doesn't get much play in our culture. That's unfortunate.

Your legacy, your mark, your fingerprints on the future are determined by the decisions you make. As we will discover with question #2, thinking in terms of legacy brings extraordinary clarity and context to the decision-making process.

Truth is, we don't know what hangs in the balance of our decisions. We can't accurately predict outcomes. But . . . and this is a big but . . . we know with certainty there are outcomes associated with each of our decisions. Even the small ones. A five-minute pause to consider generational outcomes could make all the difference.

Because we never know what hangs in the balance of

the decisions we make, we owe it to ourselves . . . and others . . . especially others . . . to consider the outcomes, the long-term outcomes. It takes a lifetime for the outcomes of some decisions to play out. In some cases, generations. For example, (and granted, this is a bit extreme): What if George Washington had decided to allow Congress to make him king? Think about the implications of that one decision. The national benefits of his decision to refuse the crown have taken generations to play out.

What if Dr. Martin Luther King Jr. had decided to stay up north and remain silent about what he knew was taking place in the South? The results of his decision to step out of his comfort zone continue to play out to this day.

I know. You aren't George Washington or Dr. King. But generations of people may very well be impacted by your decisions. In fact, if you plan on bringing children into this world, or if you've already brought children into this world, you know with certainty your personal decisions have generational implications.

Not convinced?

Let's turn it around.

Think about how different your life would be if your parents or grandparents had decided differently about a few key things. Your grandparents or parents made what seemed to them to be some small insignificant decisions, but those decisions determined the trajectory of your life, didn't they? In some cases, they determined whether or not you would even have a life. They weren't thinking about you at the time. You weren't around to be thought of.

But you have been impacted by their decisions, for better or for worse.

Perhaps your life would be very different if your dad hadn't chosen to keep picking up that bottle. You know someone whose life would be different if their momma hadn't run off and left the family.

The opposite is true as well.

Maybe your father is the one who conquered that habit and kept the family together. Maybe your mother chose to stay when another woman would have walked. The point is this: We never know what or who hangs in the balance of the decisions we make. But what we do know is this: Private decisions have public outcomes. Your private decisions probably won't stay private. Your personal decisions will impact some other persons.

I know you want to get this right. You want to write a story worth telling. I'm convinced you can.

These five questions, when asked consistently, will ensure your fingerprints on the future will be worth celebrating.

So, let's get started.

— 2 —

The Integrity Question

Am I Being Honest with
Myself . . .Really?

The easiest person to deceive is the person in the mirror.

It shouldn't be this way, but it is.

We'll talk about why in a paragraph or two. But for the moment, let that sink in. Actually, allow me to rub it in. You have talked yourself into . . . deceived yourself into . . . every bad decision you have ever made. Worse, you were the mastermind behind most of your regrettable decisions. Financial, relational, professional, academic. You were there for and willingly participated in all of 'em.

You've done more to undermine you own success and progress than anyone on the planet. Granted, there were outside pressures. Other voices. People promising you stuff. Maybe even threatening you with stuff. But in the end, you decided. But in most cases, you didn't decide by carefully weighing all the options and seeking wise counsel. You did the opposite.

In many instances, maybe even most, you knew better. Or, you should have known better. But as we touched on earlier, you ignored *know better* and started selling yourself on what yourself wanted in the moment.

It's embarrassing. We lecture kids against participating in this kind of nonsense. And I'm not pointing fingers. I participated in all my bad decisions as well. And yes, in many instances, I knew better.

So what's up?

What's up is that when it comes to good decision-making, we face our greatest challenge every morning in the mirror. Self-leadership is the greatest leadership challenge any of us face. But self-leadership is a critical component to our success in every arena of life. You'll never be a leader worth following if you don't lead yourself well. And while that's apparent if you have an official organizational leadership role, it should be equally apparent if you're a parent.

If you have children, the outcomes of your decisions are outcomes somebody you love will be forced to live with. Your self-leadership will greatly impact some other selves.

Consider this.

Whether or not you want to be like your parents depends upon how well they led themselves, not what they required of or taught you. And whether or not *your* children will want to be like you . . .

Same.

Here's why.

Exceptional self-leadership, not authority, is the key to

sustained influence. We rarely open ourselves up to the influence of people we don't respect, even if they have authority over us. So, whether we're talking about your professional life or your personal life, exceptional self-leadership is important. Your influence won't last if you don't lead yourself well first. Great leaders last because they lead themselves first.

But here's the challenge.

You can't *lead* yourself if you're *lying* to yourself.

Ever tried to lead a liar? It's pretty much impossible to lead a liar. In professional settings, you *fire* a liar. Later I'll challenge you to do just that. Fire the dishonest version of you and hire a new you . . . an honest you . . . a you that always tells you the truth, even when it makes you feel bad about you. Besides, dishonesty leaks. Lie to yourself and you'll lie to others. FYI, if you have a hard time telling other people the truth when the truth makes you look bad . . . you're probably not being honest with yourself either. It works both ways.

You know from experience that dishonesty erodes credibility and undermines moral authority. In a similar way, when we are dishonest with ourselves, it erodes credibility with ourselves. Sounds strange, I know. But when we lie out loud, what do we immediately do on the inside? In our heads?

Justify the lie.

To whom?

To ourselves.

We have to. Otherwise we are at odds with ourselves—a

state that sane people cannot maintain for long. But our internal, private justifications are . . . well . . . at best they're half-truths. Half-truths we believe! Liars lie. You're not a liar, right? So why did you lie? And off you go, creating a narrative that salvages your flailing self-esteem. And then . . . then you choose to believe it! And why would you believe a narrative you created? You are a sucker for you! You can convince yourself of just about anything.

Me too.

I played no sports in middle school or high school. Not officially, anyway. But when I was away from home and someone asked . . . particularly cute girls and athletic guys . . . if I played sports in school, I would immediately respond, "I ran track and played soccer." Technically true. I ran around the track at PE and played pick-up soccer. But that's not what they were asking and I knew it. I lied. Why? Well, you can guess. But it took me a while to get there. Looking back, I want to blame it on frontal lobe development. But the truth is . . .

The *truth* is.

More difficult to recognize than we want to admit. But admit it we must.

The truth is, in my high school, if you weren't an athlete, you just weren't. You weren't anything. Of course, that wasn't true either. But that's what it felt like. So I created a mostly false narrative and presented it whenever my flailing self-esteem felt threatened.

Author and professor Erin Brown defines a false narrative as a "Plastic Truth." She writes:

What we've said so many times in our heads becomes our Plastic Truth. Over time, these fake parts of the story—the pieces we've made up—actually cement into the gaps between Truth.

> False narratives become a crutch. We tell ourselves internal stories to avoid facing mistakes . . . It's oh-so-much easier to create a story where someone else is to blame than to confront tough things of life.[1]

Got any mostly false narratives you carry around just in case? Carry them around too long and mostly false will morph to mostly true. When that happens, you're just a few degrees away from defining yourself by a Plastic Truth.

As my AA, NA, and CA friends have repeatedly reminded me, *rigorous honesty is the first rule of recovery.* They would tell you that dishonesty fuels addictions of all kinds. Every addiction sits at the tail end of a series of decisions—decisions often fueled and protected by a false narrative, a narrative that begins as mostly true and erodes from there. Nothing changes until we are brutally honest with the person in the mirror.

So, why wait until something needs to change?

Tell yourself the truth even if it makes you feel bad about yourself.

And what do "Plastic Truth" and false narratives have to do with decision-making?

---

1. Erin M. Brown, "Why 'false narrative' is your worst enemy," https://erinbrownconroy.blog/2017/06/02/why-false-narrative-is-your-worst-enemy/

A false premise will result in a faulty decision.

You can't make the best decision *for* you until you are honest *with* you.

Furthermore, if you aren't honest about *why* you are choosing what you are choosing, you will have a difficult time taking responsibility for the outcome of your choosing. We have an adjective for people who refuse to take responsibility for their decisions:

Irresponsible.

A lack of candor in the decision-making process usually results in an inability to own the outcome. This creates a vicious downward spiral that leaves people broken and confused. Want to be broken and confused? Of course you don't. So, root out your false, plastic, mostly true self-created narratives and kiss 'em goodbye.

Well, don't kiss them.

You may find this to be more difficult than you first thought. In fact, your first step may be being honest with yourself about the fact that you're not always honest with yourself! Every journey begins with a step.

So, to decide our way into a better future, we must develop the uncomfortable habit of telling ourselves the uncomfortable truth regarding *why* we are choosing to do what we are choosing to do. Which leads us at last to the first of five questions everybody should ask every time:

Question #1: The Integrity Question

Am I being honest with myself?

You may not owe it to anyone else. But you owe it to yourself to be honest about why you choose what you choose, why you're deciding what you're deciding. There's no win in selling yourself. There's no win in justifying options.

Just tell yourself the truth.

It helps to ask this question twice. But on the second round, it helps to add a word.

- Am I being honest with myself . . . really?
- Why am I doing this . . . really?
- Why am I avoiding him . . . really?
- Why am I postponing this . . . really?
- Why do I keep making excuses . . . really?
- Why am I going . . . really?
- Why did I say yes . . . really?
- Why did I choose to wear this . . . really?
- Why did I choose to purchase, lease that . . . really?
- Why do I drive this . . . really?
- Why did I order that . . . really?
- Why did I move in . . . really?
- Why am I moving out . . . really?

As stated earlier, when it comes to selling ourselves on bad ideas or bad decisions, we're the best. When it comes to convincing ourselves to do the wrong thing, we're experts. When it comes to building and arguing a case for why we should do something we know we shouldn't do, we're unassailable litigating fools. We all deserve honorary law degrees.

So, let's stop with all that.

Just tell yourself the unfiltered truth.

It won't hurt. Well, it may hurt your ego. You may hurt your own feelings. You may embarrass yourself . . . to yourself. But in the end, it may help. Owning the real *why* behind your *what* may cause lights to come on. Lights can be terrifying. Roaches and rats certainly think so. But light can be a disinfectant. Truth can be as well. They go hand in hand. So, bring your narratives, justifications, and excuses into the light. You may learn something.

Let's start with something simple. Dessert.

Think back to your last dessert. Remember what you told yourself? "Since I didn't have dessert at lunch, a little dessert now won't hurt anything."

What?

How is that an argument for having dessert with dinner? It doesn't make sense. Most of our private justifications don't. But they don't stop us from leveraging them. A great deal of our self-talk doesn't make any sense. Don't believe me? Next time, say it out loud. When you hear the words rather than merely think the words, they take on new meaning. Actually, less meaning. They don't make sense.

Or how 'bout this one?

"I've been working hard. I deserve something sweet."

What does working hard have to do with putting something in your body you know your body would be better off without? Or this one? "I'm planning to exercise tomorrow." That's actually a reason *not* to eat dessert. You get the point.

We come into the world with a proclivity for selling ourselves on what we want to do rather than what we ought to do. I'm a sucker for me. You're a sucker for you. As soon as we see something we want, we start selling.

But all of that is just a polite way of saying, we *lie* to ourselves and believe our own lies.

Granted, an extra dessert every once in a while isn't the end of the world. Just the end of the diet. But there are decisions on which your entire future hinges. You talk yourself into *some* things and you pay. In some cases, you pay for the rest of your life.

Got a DUI or a felony conviction that raises its ugly head at the most inopportune times? An ex that keeps coming back for more money? Do you get calls from a debt collector? Don't you wish you could go back and talk yourself out of, rather than into, the decision that led to those outcomes? Sure you do. As Steven Covey famously stated:

> "You can't talk your way out of a problem you behaved your way into."

That's absolutely true. It's equally true we talked ourselves into the behavior that created the problem we're attempting to talk our way out of. Our problems usually begin when we take our own bad advice. And we're all guilty. We've all talked ourselves into things we can't talk our way out of.

THE 3 DS

Thanks to my day job, I know with certainty the three categories of decisions that create the majority of regrets:

- Purchases
- Relationships
- Habits

Oftentimes, they're related. An expensive habit can ruin a relationship. An abusive relationship can drive a person into an expensive habit. The number one cause of tension in marriage is money problems related to someone's bad financial habits.

Odds are, all your big regrets can be found in one of those three buckets. It's important to note that there are responsible purchases, mature relationships, and healthy habits. So the problem isn't the category. The problem stems from the adjective our faulty decision-making sets us up to associate with each category. We will refer to these throughout the book as the *3 Ds*.

- Dumb Purchases
- Doomed Relationships
- Destructive Habits

I'll go first.

Dumb Purchases

I'm a sucker for: "You might also like." "Customers who purchased . . . also purchased." How did they know?

How can I say no? Too often I don't. But I don't fret too much over purchasing a book I may never read, a gadget I'll rarely use, or a shirt I wear once and pass along to one of my sons. We've all made dumb purchases we laugh about later. But before I get all up in your high-regret personal purchasing business, I want you to think about the internal dialogue associated with even those harmless, affordable, spur-of-the-moment purchases. What did you tell yourself?

It wasn't like you were standing in a car dealership with a salesperson pressuring you, right? Odds are you were by yourself staring at pixels on a computer screen. You pressured yourself. You sold yourself. You convinced yourself. What did that sound like? What was your pitch? This is important. It's not important because of what you purchased. It's important for you to recognize the . . . no offense . . . juvenile logic you used to justify your purchase. It's important because the less-than-rational thought processes we use to justify harmless purchases are the same ones we use to justify the not-so-harmless ones.

I'm starting low-risk and laughable because I know you'll more readily admit to the suspect justifications you used for the blouse that wasn't exactly what you were looking for or that hard drive you didn't really need than you will that car lease you would love to find a way out of.

If an actual salesperson used the same pitch on you that you used on you, how convincing would it have been?

Not very.

You might be offended.

"If you get home and decide you don't like it, donate it."

"Just buy it; you can afford it."

"You already have one of these that does everything this one does, but this one is newer."

Everything you've purchased that you would like to bundle up and get a giant refund for . . . you sold yourself. The same is true for the large-ticket items.

The car salesman gave you information to support the decision you already wanted to make. Can't blame him. All that debt you're carrying, nobody made you flash that card. Who talked you into making that minimum payment month after month after month? You talked yourself in. You sold yourself.

But what was your pitch?

How did you do it?

How do you do it?

You should know. Because pretty soon, you'll do it again.

Are you rigorously honest with yourself when it comes to how you spend your money? I'm not concerned with what you purchase. Your business. I'm concerned about what you tell yourself before the transaction.

Listen carefully next time.

D2.

I'll speed this up.

Doomed Relationships

Perhaps you're in one right now. I hope not.

Perhaps you knew he wasn't good for you after two dates, if you could even call those dates. One part of your brain was trying to convince the other part of your brain that he wasn't the one you've been waiting on all your life. But then the other part of your brain started selling. Do you remember the pitch? Something along the lines of:

"True, he doesn't have a job. And he hasn't had a job in a while. But he's such a great guy. He's just waiting for the right opportunity. The fact that he still lives with his parents . . . he's a family guy. Yeah, that's it. He values family. And not only did he promise to pay me back, he said he would pay me back with interest. And so what if my mom doesn't approve. She's not dating him. I am!"

Imagine if a friend used that same illogic to try to talk you into going out with their brother.

"He's perfect for you. No, he's doesn't have a job. And he hasn't had one in a while . . ."

I'll spare you.

Pretty much everything on the pitch list would register negative coming from someone else's lips. But when it originates in our minds, somehow it's different. And that makes it dangerous.

Guys?

"True, she can be manipulative. And she's admitted that she's not good with money. She's constantly texting her old boyfriend. Says she owes him money. But she's fun. And you've seen her, right? She has great taste in restaurants . . . expensive taste . . . but I think that's because she appreciates quality."

Again, if anybody other than you used that pitch on you . . .

Looking back, we wonder how we missed the signs. How

could we have been so clueless? But the problem isn't that we're clueless. The problem is, like any good sales associate, we assist ourselves in seeing what we want to see . . . while ignoring all the warning lights flashing right in front of us.

More on why later.

Destructive Habits

Then, of course, there are those destructive habits.

If you don't have any or know anybody who has any, feel free to skip this part.

Remember the first time you . . . whatever it is you do that you can't seem to stop. Do you remember what the salesperson inside of you whispered? I do, and I wasn't even there: "You can handle this." Followed by some version of, "Don't worry, you'll always be the master, you'll never be mastered." And you believed you. But what began as a pleasurable pastime, turned out to be a pathway. A pathway that led to a habit. Perhaps an addiction. An addiction that may have been avoided . . . like that doomed relationship and those unwise purchasing decisions . . . if you had paused and asked: Am I being honest with myself . . . really? Why am I doing this . . . really?

The sentence following this sentence is so important I added it to make sure you didn't read past it too quickly.

You rarely have to sell yourself on a *good* idea.

You rarely have to sell yourself on the right thing to do, the healthy thing to do, the responsible thing to do. You just know. Good ideas rarely need any defense. When you start selling yourself, you need to hit the pause button and ask, "Am I being completely honest with myself . . . really? If so, why am I selling myself so hard?" The wise thing to do is usually so compelling it doesn't need selling.

Here's how it works:

Our hearts get wrapped around something or someone and we experience desire. Want. So the heart sends a message to the brain: "Hey brain, I want this. Figure out a way to justify it and get it for me." Now our brains are smart. That's why we call them brains. And our brains know that whereas it's difficult to justify a *want*, it's not so difficult to justify a *need*. So the first thing the brain does is upgrade the messaging to something far more sophisticated than *want*. The brain says: "You NEED this."

Once we're convinced we NEED something, it's easy to sell ourselves on it. Before long, we have a list of justifications for buying it, drinking it, staying, leaving, lying, asking it out, or asking it in. But the reasons we use to sell ourselves aren't really reasons. They're *justifications*. Justifications for what we want to do. So, here's a second version of the same idea I highlighted above.

You rarely have to *justify* a *good* idea.

Justifying is akin to just-a-lying. You're just-a-lying to yourself. And in most instances you know it. But we listen to our convoluted, confused reasoning until we actually believe it. And once that starts, it's so hard to be honest with ourselves, isn't it? There's always an internal conflict between the options we intuitively know we should choose and the options we are tempted to choose, between the options that are best for us and the options we sell ourselves on.

Again, when it comes to selling ourselves on bad ideas, we're amazing, which is so odd, because at the same time, we are all 100 percent committed to what's best for us. At least in our minds. But not always in our decisions. Do you want to be healthy? Of course you do. We all do. But we all decide to the contrary just about every time we sit down to eat. Do you want to be healthy financially and relationally? Of course you do. Again, we all do. Why, then, are we so prone to decide in the opposite direction?

Why is self-control so difficult for ourselves when ourselves would swear we want what's best for ourselves.

Strange, isn't it?

We've all stared at ourselves in the mirror and asked, "Why did I do that?" "Again." Another way of asking the same question is, "Why did I decide to do that again?" Which leads us to a question I want us to tackle as we wrap up this chapter.

Why *are* we so prone to self-deception?

Why do we lie to ourselves?

Why do we lie to ourselves about ourselves?

Why do we talk ourselves into things we later regret?

Most importantly, how do we stop?

First why, then how.

FILTERS

When it comes to *why* we have a hard time telling ourselves the truth, psychologists suggest it's not really 100 percent our fault.

Got to love psychologists.

Apparently, we are all victims of a cognitive bias dubbed confirmation bias. Confirmation bias is the tendency we all have to look for information or arguments that support what we already believe and reasons that support what we are already inclined to do. Confirmation bias empowers us to see what we want to see and hear what we want to hear. Confirmation bias empowers us to tune out everything to the contrary. Seeking information to confirm our assumptions comes naturally. Proactively looking for or even being open to information to the contrary is unusual. Unnatural. If we want something to be true badly enough, the stars magically align. In our minds, anyway. And information to the contrary gets filtered out. Not only are we not objective, we burn calories not to be objective. We handcuff ourselves to our assumptions and prejudices.

The United States is currently divided over three issues about which you probably have an opinion: abortion, gun control, and climate change. Not emotionally neutral subjects for most people. To my knowledge, there is no secret information regarding these three topics. The stats, history, and science are out there for anybody who is interested in discovering them. If you're honest . . . which is the point of this chapter . . . you have probably never proactively sought out information contrary to the opinion you hold on these three hot issues. Right? But when you bump into something that supports your view, you're all about it! You pass it along to a friend. You post the link.

The moral of the story is . . . and you're going to hate

me for this . . . most of us want to be proven *right* more than we want to know what's *true*. We aren't on truth quests. We're on confirmation quests.

Confirmation bias explains in part why moms and their daughters arrive at opposite conclusions about the same boy. Theists look at nature and conclude design and a designer while nontheists see neither. For Democrats, President Obama could do no wrong. For Republicans, everything he did was wrong.

Of course, *neither* was correct.

That probably triggered your confirmation bias.

Sneaky.

For the record, even President Obama admitted he made mistakes. For the record, every president makes mistakes. But while a president is in office, our confirmation bias is louder than any political or cultural reality. And that won't change. And that probably won't hurt you. But on a personal level, wanting to be proven right more than wanting to know what's true will undermine your ability to make good decisions. Worse, it pretty much guarantees bad decisions. A confirmation quest is a dangerous quest. It will blind you to what can hurt you. It sets you up to freely, cheerfully, and confidently choose the wrong option.

Everyone is a potential victim of confirmation bias. The folks who escape its clutches are the exceptional people who recognize what's happening and go looking for information that doesn't line up with their biases. That is a rare individual. It requires extraordinary security and an uncommon measure of curiosity.

NOTHING NEW

The term "confirmation bias" was first used by English psychologist Peter Watson in the 1960s. But this trait has been observed for much longer. Francis Bacon, another Englishman, made the following observation in the seventeenth century:

> The human understanding when it has once adopted an opinion . . . draws all things else to support and agree with it. And though there be a greater number and weight of instances to be found on the other side, yet these it either neglects or despises, or else by some distinction sets aside or rejects.[2]

The Greek historian Thucydides, as far back as the fourth century BC, observed:

> . . . for it is a habit of mankind to entrust to careless hope what they long for, and to use sovereign reason to thrust aside what they do not fancy.[3]

But hundreds of years before Thucydides, in the seventh century BC, a court advisor turned prophet made a similar observation. The context of his observation is both fascinating and instructive.

---

2. *Novum Organum*, Francis Bacon, 1620.
3. *The Peloponnesian War.*

HEART HEALTH

Jeremiah served as advisor to a series of kings who ruled the ancient kingdom of Judah, kings whose careers would've gone much smoother and whose lives would have been extended if they had listened to Jeremiah's advice. But of course the advantage, perhaps the point, of being king is that you don't have to listen to anyone's advice!

Jeremiah's challenging career began as advisor to young King Jehoiakim. Israel had recently become a puppet state, paying an annual financial tribute to Babylon, who in return provided military assistance while allowing Israel to conduct her own affairs. After three years, King Jehoiakim determined he'd had enough of that, and decided to withhold his tribute and declare his allegiance to Babylon's archrival, Egypt. When Jeremiah got wind of Jehoiakim's plans, he warned the king of the consequences of rebelling against the mighty Nebuchadnezzar, who had recently been defeated by the Egyptian army and was already in a really foul military mood. But Jehoiakim wouldn't listen.

To put this in perspective, this would be akin to the smallest town in your state declaring war on the United States.

Pointless and dangerous.

Jeremiah assured the king that not only was this a bad idea, it was in direct opposition to God's will for the nation at that time. Jehoiakim wasn't concerned about that either. He had long since abandoned the ways of Judaism. Rabbinical writings describe King Jehoiakim as a merciless tyrant whose sexual appetites led him far outside the moral prohibitions outlined in Jewish law. Besides, by the time Jeremiah got to him, he had already made up his mind.

He did exactly what he had already planned to do.

Sure enough, King Nebuchadnezzar did exactly what Jeremiah predicted he would do as well.

In 598 BC, Nebuchadnezzar invaded Judah and laid siege to the city of Jerusalem. The siege lasted three months, after which Nebuchadnezzar's army entered the city, bound Jehoiakim in chains, and marched him back to Babylon, adding him to his king collection.

That's right. Nebuchadnezzar collected kings.

Literally, he collected living kings. Some people collect coins. King Nebuchadnezzar collected kings. When he conquered a nation, he would capture the king alive and bring him to join his collection. On special occasions, when he wanted to show off just how powerful he was, he would bring 'em out in gold chains and parade them around the courtroom. Each king would walk with his hand on the shoulder of the king in front of him . . . because in addition to being in chains, King Nebuchadnezzar had them all blinded.

Back to our story line.

Before leaving Jerusalem, King Nebuchadnezzar crowned Jehoiakim's son Jehoiachin king. He was eighteen years old. But just three months later, Nebuchadnezzar changed his mind, sent for the recently coronated Jehoiachin, and added him to his collection as well. Along with the newly appointed king, Nebuchadnezzar had his generals bring back ten thousand captives from the upper class of Jerusalem and the surrounding area, including the entire royal family. In addition, he rounded up and imprisoned the nation's military leaders. Then, as a final measure to ensure Judah would never again consider breaking away from Babylonian rule, he ordered his men to plunder the palace and treasury.

As you might imagine, at this point nobody with any sense was anxious to be the next king of Judah. But every kingdom needs a king, so Nebuchadnezzar appointed Jehoiachin's uncle, Zedekiah, king. He was twenty-one. What young King Zedekiah didn't know . . . what nobody knew . . . was that he would be the last king of Judah. Like the kings before him, he would not listen to sound advice. Like those previous kings, he took his own counsel and listened only to the voices that echoed that counsel. One Jewish historian had this to say about young King Zedekiah:

> He did evil in the eyes of the LORD his God and did not humble himself before Jeremiah the prophet.[4]

No sooner did Nebuchadnezzar head back to Babylon when the newly coronated King Zedekiah chose to do exactly as King Jehoiakim had done—declared independence from Babylon.

Jeremiah pleaded with Zedekiah not to repeat the mistakes of the past. He warned the king that maintaining

---

4. 2 Chronicles 36:12.

his current position would result in the destruction of the city as well as the king's family. But kings will be kings. Zedekiah ignored Jeremiah and listened instead to those around him, who heralded him as the savior of the city and the kingdom. Jeremiah responded by taking his message to the streets.

He assured the citizens of Jerusalem that rebellion would result in their destruction. He encouraged the population to open the gates to the Babylonians, and that if they did, they would be spared. When Zedekiah heard what Jeremiah was doing, he instructed his bodyguard to put Jeremiah in a dry cistern to get him out of the way and to silence him.

He was scaring the children.

Actually, he was scaring the entire population.

In the ninth year of his reign, Zedekiah entered into an alliance with Egypt. This was essentially a declaration of war with Babylon. As Jeremiah predicted, Nebuchadnezzar himself led his army to crush the rebellion. The Babylonian army laid siege to the city once again in an effort to starve the inhabitants into submission. When King Zedekiah realized how foolish he'd been and how hopeless the situation truly was, he called for Jeremiah and begged him to ask God to deliver the city. Jeremiah assured the king that it was too late for that. Their fate had been sealed. Their only hope was to throw open the gates, surrender the city, and submit to King Nebuchadnezzar. Zedekiah knew what that meant for him and his family. So, he refused and instead attempted to sneak out of the city with his bodyguard and his children.

He was quickly captured and forced to watch as his children were cut down one by one by Nebuchadnezzar's guards. And that would be the last thing Zedekiah would ever see. He was blinded, wrapped in golden chains, and added to Nebuchadnezzar's king collection in Babylon.

NOT US!

When you read or hear a story like that, you can't help but wonder, *Really?* You can't help but think, *Not me!* With everything at stake . . . including the lives of his family, why wouldn't he listen? You wouldn't have to be a prophet to know resistance was futile.

Interestingly enough, it was during his interaction with stubborn King Zedekiah that Jeremiah documented his version of why we, like King Jehoiachin and King Zedekiah, are so prone toward self-deception—why we, too, are so good at selling ourselves on bad options in spite of ample and convincing evidence to the contrary. Here's what he wrote:

The heart is *deceitful* above all things . . .[5]

The heart, as in *every* heart. Your heart. My heart. The heart is deceitful. Jeremiah chose his adjective carefully. As you know, there's a difference between dishonest and deceitful. Dishonest is easier to spot than deceitful, isn't

---

5. Jeremiah 17:9.

it? Dishonest is just straight up not honest. But deceitful? Deceitful implies an agenda. Deceitful usually includes a mix of truth, half-truth, and untruth. If our hearts straight up lied to us all the time, that would be easy to catch. But deceitful? Deceitful is more difficult to detect.

You've met dishonest people who weren't shrewd enough to deceive you. Their dishonesty was apparent. But deceitful people? They're the dangerous ones. Again, Jeremiah chose his words carefully. Our hearts are deceitful. They can be dangerous. It's why we're so *convinced* and at times so *convincing.* We don't merely lie to ourselves; we deceive ourselves.

But Jeremiah wasn't done.

> The heart is deceitful above all things
>   and *beyond* cure.

There's no cure. It's a permanent condition. We don't outgrow it. We don't outmature it. We can't fix it. It's hardwired. We're doomed!

Well, we're not doomed.

But . . .

A permanent condition requires constant supervision. A permanent condition requires a proactive response. Otherwise, we will deceive ourselves. But before we get to that . . . Jeremiah is still not finished. He wraps up by stating something we've all experienced. Especially looking back and wondering how we could've been so *deceived*, how we could have decided so poorly.

> The heart is deceitful above all things
>   and beyond cure.
>   Who can *understand* it?

Good question.

Not me.

Apparently, nobody.

This explains why we've all said at some point, "I don't *understand* why I did what I did." Which is just another way of saying, "I don't understand why I *decided* what I decided." "Chose what I chose." It's why we do things that make perfect sense in the moment that make utterly no sense a moment later. It explains why you decided to do the very thing you advised someone else *not* to do earlier. It's why the person in the mirror is the most difficult person you will ever attempt to lead. They don't tell the truth.

Unless you force them to.

You've got to pin 'em down, look 'em in the eye, and ask, "Are you being honest with me? Really?"

Jeremiah's words explain why smart people make not-so-smart decisions.

Decisions we look at and think, *Even I would know better than to do that!* But would we? Would we if it were us listening to our smart selves? Probably not.

I've watched intelligent, resourced men that had worked hard to amass significant wealth, lose a significant portion of it on an "investment" that was really just a scheme . . . a scheme that promised more of what they already had, only quicker this time. When I listen to their stories, I think,

How did someone as smart and as successful as you fall for something as dubious as that? After the fact, they wonder the same thing. In the moment . . . well . . . in the moment they were just like us. Deceived. Their hearts were deceitful. Mine is too.

So is yours.

THE WAY FORWARD

So, if there's no cure, if we never graduate from or mature past this, if we will always have a propensity to deceive ourselves, talk ourselves into the very thing we should talk ourselves out of, sell ourselves *on* the very things we should declare off-limits, what then do we do? Sounds pretty hopeless, doesn't it?

Well, while it's true there's no cure, there is hope. There is a way to keep our deceitful hearts in check. Here are three tips.

To begin with, *admit it.*

The sooner you embrace this uncomfortable, disquieting fact about yourself, the quicker you'll be able to develop and maintain a healthy suspicion. The more open you'll be to information and advice that conflicts with where your heart is taking you. The more cautious you will be when the salesman inside you starts selling you. The easier it will be to recognize what you are tempted to justify may be just a lie you're telling yourself.

Second, *ask it.*

Ask our question: Am I being honest with myself . . . really?

Have a heart-to-heart with yourself. Have it in the mirror. Look yourself in the eye. Seriously, stand in front of the mirror and ask yourself out loud . . . and use your name. "Andy, are you being honest with yourself . . . really?" And then, tell yourself the truth even . . . even . . . if you don't plan to *act* on it.

You owe it to yourself to *know*, even if knowing points you in a direction you don't intend to go.

It won't hurt to know. You need to be honest with yourself . . . really.

Third, *be curious*.

Echoing the prophet Jeremiah, Brené Brown insists, "Our rational, grown-up selves are good liars."[6] To punch through our deceptive selves requires what she refers to as "emotional curiosity." When we push through our discomfort and get curious about *why* we're feeling what we're feeling . . . why we are determined to do what we are hell-bent on doing, we get to the truth.

But most people don't do that.

Don't be most people.

Be curious. Curiosity will keep you focused on the frontiers of your ignorance. That's where we learn. That's where we gain insight. It's where we catch sight of our prejudice and our narrow-mindedness. When it's uncomfortable . . . and it will get uncomfortable. When it gets uncomfortable

---

6. Brené Brown, *Rising Strong: How the Ability to Reset Transforms the Way We Live, Love, Parent, and Lead* (New York: Random House, 2015), 86.

and you are tempted to turn away . . . to turn back to what you've always known, know this . . . that is fear talking. That is insecurity talking. You'll learn little from either. So turn back around and be curious. If you do, you will learn something. If nothing else, you will learn something about yourself.

We naturally resist what we don't understand and what we can't control. We are always tempted to dismiss and excuse and criticize what we don't understand and can't control. When we do, we lose. As I tell leaders all the time, be a student, not a critic. Critics look for reasons not to learn from what they don't understand. Students, on the other hand, are always learning. They face their ignorance. They are curious. Be curious. Ask yourself, "Why am I doing this, really? Why did I react the way I did when confronted with new insight and information? Why did I bristle when questioned? Why won't I read that book, that article?"

WHY WE DON'T

As simple as all this sounds, it's not simple. It's terrifying. After all, once we're honest with ourselves, we're accountable—accountable to ourselves. This means when we hear ourselves giving our friends and family all the "reasons" we've come up with to support our really bad decisions, we'll know we're lying.

"The reason I went . . ."

"The reason I bought it . . ."

"The reason I called her . . ."

"The reason I called him back . . ."

"The reason we're moving . . ."

"The reason I'm moving in . . ."

Once you've been absolutely honest with yourself, it's gonna be a bit harder to be dishonest with everybody else. And while being honest with ourselves can be a bit terrifying, being honest with ourselves, telling ourselves the truth, can be . . . liberating. In fact, it's almost always liberating. Jesus made a powerful statement in this regard. You may not know Jesus said it because politicians say it all the time . . . without giving Jesus credit. Apparently, it's okay to mention what Jesus says as long as you don't mention Jesus.

Jesus said, *"You will know the truth, and the truth will set you free."*

The truth really will set you free. But the opposite is true as well: dishonesty will imprison you. And if we're not careful, we'll imprison ourselves when we're less than honest with ourselves.

Telling yourself the truth, owning up to the real reason you're considering what you're considering, will bring immediate clarity. You will see better. It will be harder to deceive yourself. In this way, telling yourself the truth will empower you to make the right decision. And that's why you've got to ask it. Twice.

Am I being honest with myself . . . really?

Am I telling myself the truth or selling myself a regret?

As we close, I want to ask a series of questions. Most of these won't have anything to do with your current situation. But perhaps one or two of them will. These are the kinds of questions we should all get in the habit of asking. Odds are, nobody's around. And even if they are, they can't read your mind. So, there's no reason not to be honest. I'll even give you an out: You don't have to *do* anything. Just be honest with yourself. Okay?

Ready?

Not the excuse you've been telling yourself and your friends. The real reason.

Why are you buying . . . ?

Why are you moving?

Why do you continue to go out with him? Her? Really?

Why did you file for divorce . . . really?

What's the real reason you moved in?

Why are you taking that job . . . really?

What's the real reason you don't call your kids? Your mom? Your dad? Your brother or sister?

Brutal, isn't it?

Terrifying.

Clarifying.

Hopefully, liberating and empowering.

Throughout our lives, we will be forced to make decisions we don't really want to make. All of them will be made in some sort of emotional context. There are no emotionally neutral decision-making environments. Because of that, we will be prone to opt for happy now over healthy later. Pleasure over self-control. Because our hearts are deceitful, because of confirmation bias, we will be prone to talk ourselves into things we will regret later.

But it doesn't have to be that way.

It doesn't have to continue to be that way.

There's a way out of that destructive cycle. And although we've never met, I bet there's something in you that wants out. So, take a baby step. Start being brutally honest with yourself. Quit lying to yourself. Refuse to make up reasons that are actually justifications. When you catch yourself selling yourself, just stop and say, "There I go again." Pause to have a heart-to-heart with yourself by asking, "Why am I doing this? Why am I doing this, really?"

COMMITTED

To help you adopt our first question as part of your decision-making filter, I want to encourage you to make a specific and pointed decision. I'll conclude each chapter with a similar decision. But this one may be the most important one and perhaps the most difficult one to keep.

Decision #1: The Integrity Decision
I will not lie to myself even when the truth
makes me feel bad about myself.

Pardon my presumption, but you may need to write that down and put it where you can see it every day. For a while anyway. I suggest a mirror.

There are worse things than feeling bad about yourself. For starters, clinging to something bad about yourself. Refusing to address what's bad about ourselves is bad for ourselves. Are you willing to be honest with yourself even if it makes you feel bad about yourself? You'll never get to where you need to be until you acknowledge where you actually are to begin with. So be honest.

Jeremiah was right: "The heart is deceitful above all things and beyond cure."

But now you know.

And now you know what to do about it.

Now you're better equipped to make better decisions and live with fewer regrets. Which is a good thing. After all, your decisions determine the direction and quality of your life as well as the lives of those you love.

Are you being honest with yourself?

Really?

Ready for question #2?

Really?

— 3 —

The Legacy Question

What Story Do I Want to Tell?

Every decision you make becomes a permanent part of your story.

The story of your life.

What story do *you* want to tell?

What story do you want told *about* you?

The good news is, you get to decide. But you decide one decision at a time, because you write the story of your life . . . one decision at a time.

I was fortunate to grow up with a dad who took his responsibility as a father seriously. My dad's dad died when my dad was seventeen months old. His mom didn't remarry until he was in high school. For all practical purposes, he grew up without a father. Experts say the first six years are the most critical ones as it relates to personal development. My dad's mom did the best she could under the circumstances. And circumstances were harsh in the thirties and forties in Dry Fork, Virginia.

Difficult circumstances make or break folks. In my father's case, it made him fiercely independent, disciplined, and determined to create something better for his family— which he certainly did. But not just in the ways you might expect. My sister and I certainly grew up in a more stable financial environment. But my dad was equally determined to make sure we had the relationship he missed, the one that, in his words, left a "deep enduring void" in his heart. My father was determined to be a good dad. To be present and accounted for. To give us the relationship he never had.

And he did.

No role model. No lessons. No parenting seminars. He just figured it out.

One of the most significant things he did was to lie down beside us at night as we were drifting off to sleep. After we prayed, I would start asking questions. Of course the questions were a stall tactic. I didn't want him to leave. It's funny. As I'm writing this not only can I still picture my bedroom, I can almost smell it. It had a distinct smell. It was a cross between my old brown bedspread and my alligator.

I had a pet alligator named Wally.

He or she . . . never was able to figure that out . . . lived in an aquarium in my bedroom. Most of the time. Occasionally Wally would manage to get out. I always knew when my alligator was out. I would come home from school and my bedroom door would be shut with a towel shoved underneath. That was my cue to slip in as quickly as possible and find Wally.

Anyway.

Prayer time would quickly transition to story time. But not bedtime stories. For whatever reason, I was always fascinated by my dad's stories, what life was like for him as a kid. I was particularly interested in what he got in trouble for. I remember most of them because when he ran out of stories, I would ask him to retell particular ones. Years later, I would tell my kids my dad's stories. Delivering newspapers at 5:00 a.m. before he walked to school. Breaking customers' windows with frozen newspapers because they weighed too much and he threw too hard.

Coming home to an empty house every afternoon because his mom didn't finish at the textile mill until 5:00 p.m. and she rode the bus home. Fixing his own breakfast in the mornings because his mom was already at the bus stop.

When we were old enough to understand, he described his arduous and sometimes violent relationship with his stepfather who married my dad's mom when my dad was in high school. Henry was an angry man who took it out on my grandmother . . . until my dad was old enough and big enough to intervene. There was the story of how he eventually sold his paper route, which provided enough money to consider college. He told us about the chance conversation with a friend that led to a conversation with a friend of a friend that landed him a full scholarship.

He showed up at the University of Richmond with a suitcase and less than $30.00 to his name. I loved the story of how he met my mom, the rich girl from Smithfield, North Carolina.

As a kid I discovered quickly that my dad's story had an additional layer—his grandfather's story.

His grandfather, George Washington Stanley . . . I didn't make that up . . . was from Siler City, North Carolina, best known for being the home of Frances Bavier, better known as Aunt Bee on *The Andy Griffith Show*. George Stanley was an uneducated Pentecostal holiness preacher leading up to, during, and following the days of prohibition in America. His stories were like something out of a movie—fire and brimstone sermons, death threats, gangsters in burning cars. My dad spent one summer with his grandfather that marked him for life and would eventually leave a dent in me as well. Every afternoon after work, they would sit on George's front porch sipping lemonade and talking about life. George's life. His life philosophy was simple and unforgettable. I've heard my dad repeat it a thousand times.

"Obey God and leave all the consequences to him. If God tells you to run your head through a brick wall, start running and trust God to make a hole."

As I write this, my dad is about to celebrate his eighty-seventh birthday. But those stories, his stories and my grandfather's stories, are as vivid as they were the first times I heard 'em. But, it wasn't just his childhood stories that impacted me. As his son, I've had a ringside seat for some of the most important stories in his story. And as is the case with every father and son, his stories become my stories. They were immediately grafted into the story of my life. Again, as is the case with every father, his choices influenced my choices. His decisions influenced the direction and quality of my life.

Particularly his decision to take a job in Atlanta when I was in the fifth grade. It was a difficult and somewhat risky decision that determined so much of the trajectory of my life, career, and marriage.

What I didn't grasp as a child but is abundantly clear to me now is that my father's story is simply a series of outcomes connected to a series of decisions. In many cases, decisions made in response to other people's decisions. He was writing the story of his life one decision at a time. He was writing chapters in the story of my life, one decision at a time. And while there are no perfect stories, he certainly wrote a good one. One worth telling.

One worth retelling.

The above example illustrates and intersects with something we touched on in the previous chapter. We never know what or who hangs in the balance of the decisions we make, and thus the stories we tell. What we *do* know is that private decisions have public implications. Perhaps generational implications. Our private decisions won't remain private. Our personal decisions will impact other persons. I never met my great grandfather. But his decisions, which created his story, would eventually intersect with his great grandson.

STORIES

We don't think this way, do we?

We don't think of our lives as stories—stories we will tell or stories that will be told about us.

If my father's stepfather had known his stepson would grow up to be a world famous pastor, author, and speaker, he may have opted for a better story. He might have decided to treat him better. If it had occurred to him that some day his stepson would tell his story and that his story would include his interactions with his stepfather, perhaps he would have decided differently. So it bears repeating. Our *private* decisions don't remain *private*. Our *personal* decisions impact other *persons*. Once our story becomes their story, it is *their* story to tell.

Which brings us to our second question.

Question #2: The Legacy Question
What story do you want to tell?

While I'm asking, what story do you want told?

Every decision you make, every decision becomes a permanent part of your story. The story of your life. Every decision you make has an outcome, a consequence, a result. It may be good or bad. Desirable, undesirable. Expected, unexpected. Whatever the case, that outcome becomes a permanent part of the story of your life.

> You went out with him. He was a jerk. But he was cute. And he was convenient. And there wasn't anybody else on the horizon. Two years later, the whole thing just evaporated. You saw it coming, but felt stuck.

Now part of your story is that you wasted two years of your life dating in a relationship with someone that you knew early on was . . . well . . . wasn't the one.

> Your boss asked you to lie to a client. You're not a liar, but you lied. The client called you on it. Your boss threw you under the bus. You lost your job.

Now, part of your story is that you lied and lost your job over it. The better story would have been, *You refused to lie and lost your job over it.*

> Your friends wanted to go out. You had an exam the next day. You told your friends no. They pressed. You pressed back and stayed in your dorm. You aced the exam and now you have a diploma with an honors sticker to show for it.

You'll never forget that night. Meanwhile, your college friends are . . . well . . . you're not sure where they are.

Decision by decision, you are writing the story of your life. So, when you're making a decision of any magnitude, you owe it to yourself to pause, look ahead, and ask yourself: "What story do I want to tell?"

Here's another angle.

The decisions you're in the middle of making right now . . . this week . . . today . . . are going to be reduced to a story you tell. Once it's behind you, it's a story. Period. If you lost your job recently, surviving this season without a job is going to be a story you tell someday.

What story do you want to tell?

> I lost my job. I was embarrassed. I told friends I was doing consulting work. But I wasn't *consulting*; I was *consoling* myself every afternoon with a bottle. I racked up a ton of debt. I lost the respect of my wife and kids. Maybe worse, I lost my self-respect.

That's not a good story. Losing a job . . . going for a prolonged period of time without meaningful work is terrifying and demeaning. But . . . the decisions one makes in the valleys are eventually just stories they tell on the other side. Write a good story.

Decide a good story.

Perhaps you're dating someone and things are going really well, but there's someone else at the office who's caught your eye. She's married. In spite of that, you find yourself gravitating in her direction, primarily because she seems to be gravitating in yours as well. Eventually she makes it clear that if you're willing, she's willing. Sounds fun. But your decision becomes part of your story. A permanent part.

What story do you want to tell?

> I got involved with a married woman at work. I lied to my girlfriend . . . I busted this woman's marriage. Now her kids ping-pong between two homes on the weekends.

Is that really the story you want to tell? I don't think so. In fact, that would be a story you hope nobody finds out about.

The challenge is, most of us don't think this way. Life as story. Though we've probably never met, here's something I know about you: You would like to be able to tell your entire story without skipping any chapters or having to lie about the details.

Right?

Someday, you would like to be able to sit down or lie down with your kids or grandkids and tell 'em your story. Your entire story. And as they get older, you would like to be able to add layers and details rather than hoping they don't ask.

If you're single, you want to someday sit across the table from someone you hope to spend the rest of your life with and tell your story. All of it. You'd like to be the hero in your own story. We all want that. And going forward, you can have that. But it will require you to stop mid-decision and ask: "What story do I want to tell? When this crisis, this opportunity, this temptation is in the rearview mirror . . . when it's reduced to a story I tell . . . what story do I want to tell?" Which of the available options do you want as part of your story?

THE FOG OF NOW

The primary reason we don't think in terms of *story* when making decisions is that *story* is later. Decisions are *now*. We think about later, later. As in later when it's too *late* to do anything about it. We don't think in terms of story because we're distracted by the pressure and emotions we feel in the moment.

Emotion is like a fog.

It causes us to lose sight of the broader context. Namely, our stories.

You know how this works. You're up against a deadline. You've got to decide and you've got to decide soon!

"If you won't marry me, I'm leaving."

Nobody wants to be left.

"If you don't make your quota, you're fired."

Nobody wants to be fired.

When we're under pressure, it's hard to think about tomorrow, much less the story we're going to tell. We've got to get through today. Whether it's love, lust, jealousy, insecurity, fear . . . emotions complicate the decision-making process by focusing our attention on the immediate rather than the ultimate. We're left thinking in terms of our options and choices, but not our stories. Immediate outcomes, not ultimate outcomes.

If we flip it around, it gets even clearer. Maybe too clear.

Isn't it true that your worst decisions were fueled by something with strong emotional appeal? Not rational . . . emotional. That weekend. That first marriage. That purchase. That lease. It was so appealing, you bought it. It was so appealing, you ate it. It was so appealing, you dated it and moved in with it. It was so appealing, you jumped at the opportunity. It was so appealing, you took it, smoked it. . . . It goes on and on. The reason we have regrets, the reason we look back and wonder, What was I thinking? is because we were presented with something that had strong emotional appeal.

If you're in sales, you know how this works. And you know that about the worst thing you can do is let a potential customer leave the store or showroom without making a sale. Once they walk out, what happens? The emotional attachment they felt toward your product begins to lessen. They gain perspective. They're far less likely to purchase your product.

Psychologists have a name for this dynamic. It's another cognitive bias. It explains why once our appetites are engaged in the decision-making process, we . . . well . . . to some degree we lose our minds. We lose our ability to think rationally, or, as rationally. This particular cognitive bias has been labeled *focalism* because victims hyper focus on one thing to the neglect of everything in the vicinity.

If you've ever been in love, you've been a victim of focalism.

Focalism, or *anchoring* as it's sometimes referred to,

is the tendency we all have to rely too heavily on initial information and the emotion it elicits when making a decision. The initial information, enhanced by the accompanying feelings, becomes larger than life and taints or blurs other facts and bits of information that should be taken into consideration. Essentially, we lose focus of our surroundings, our decision-making context, and hyper *focus* on the thing, opportunity, option, or person in front of us.

When you fell in love, all you could see was him.

All you could think about was her.

Everything else faded into the background. Including his credit card debt and her dating history. When focalism kicks in, and it kicks in more frequently than you might imagine, everything except the thing we're fixated on is blurred by comparison. Including the future. Our stories. After all, in emotionally charged decision-making environments, we think in terms of choices, not stories, which means we aren't doing our best thinking.

So here's a tip.

When confronted with anything or anybody that has strong emotional appeal, press pause, not play. Strong emotional appeal should trigger a red flag, not a green light. When something is emotionally appealing, instead of leaning in, we should step back. Not because he's not the one. He may be. Not because it's not a good investment. It may be. Not because it's not the perfect job. It may be. We should step back because anything with strong emotional appeal . . . even the right thing . . . clouds our judgment.

So pause. Get your bearings. Go home and think about it. Call a friend. Consider your story.

Considering your story positions and empowers you to counteract the effects of *focalism*. This alone makes the question, "What story do I want to tell?" worth asking. It draws us out of the immediate and focuses on the eventual. It empowers us to put the decision-making process within the broader context of the story of our lives. Our stories are future tense. So every decision should be made with this question in mind:

What story do I want to tell?

NOT THE FIRST

We're not the first generation to wrestle with question. And while there are endless examples of people in history who got this wrong and people who got this right, there is one particular narrative from the past that perfectly illustrates the benefits and consequences of both. It, too, is found in the Jewish Scripture. But unlike the story of Jeremiah and Zedekiah from chapter one, this ancient story is a familiar one. I chose this bit of narrative because it not only illustrates the power of this question, but the primary character models a specific application of this idea I have found to be extraordinarily helpful.

But first, some context.

Around 1850 BC, a Hebrew teenager named Joseph found himself in a tough spot. His father, Jacob, loved him more than he loved Joseph's eleven brothers. The reason for the preferential treatment was that Joseph had been born to Jacob in his old age and he was the son of Jacob's favorite wife.

It's best not to have a favorite wife.

Anyway.

The narrative picks up steam when Jacob assigns Joseph with the task of checking on his brothers and bringing back a report. This had happened before. Joseph's previous report wasn't very good. And apparently the bad report left them in an even worse standing with Dad. So this time when the brothers see Joseph headed their way, they *decide* to act on something they've been feeling for a long time.

They decide to kill him.

But as Joseph gets closer, they lose their nerve and decided instead to throw him into an empty well . . . until they can get up the nerve to kill him.

And you thought your siblings were merciless.

You may remember this story from childhood. If so, you'll remember that Joseph gets a break. Sort of. Instead of killing him, Joseph's brothers decide to sell him.

Way more profitable.

A bit more merciful.

They sell him to slave traders for a wholesale price, knowing the slave traders will sell him again in Egypt at retail. Of course, they would have to explain Joseph's disappearance and so they fabricated a tale to cover their crime. They took Joseph's coat, the famous one, the one his father had fashioned especially for Joseph, and dipped it in goat's blood. Then they made their way home feigning grief over the death of their brother, apparently by way of the claws and jaws of a wild beast.

Jacob's heart is broken.

Joseph's older brothers have a secret they would be forced to live with for the rest of their lives. Their lie made them liars for life.

I want to pause the story here for a moment.

Imagine if we could've dropped in on Joseph's brothers as they were contemplating how to channel their misplaced jealousy. What if we could have asked them our question:

Hey guys, what story do you want to tell?

How you choose to treat your younger brother is eventually going to be nothing more than a story you tell. Depending on what you do, it may be a secret you keep. But it will be a permanent part of your story.

So before you do something extreme, do you really want your story to be, "When I was in my twenties, I was so jealous of my younger brother, since my father loved his mother more than he loved my mother . . . and therefore loved my younger brother more than he loved me, which come to think of it, has nothing to do with my younger brother . . . who I hate. It's really my dad's fault. Anyway, when I was in my twenties, I hated my younger brother so much that I sold him into slavery and then told my dad he was killed by wild animals. Then I spent the rest of my life lying about what happened to my younger brother all because I was jealous."

Guys, is that really the story you want to tell? Seriously? For the rest of your life? Do you really want a chapter you're ashamed of? That you hope nobody ever finds out about?

I don't know. Joseph's brothers may have reconsidered. Maybe not. But when you look at their options from the perspective of story, the option they opted for looks . . . well . . . small. Petty. An overreaction for sure. More mob mentality than thoughtful consideration. If you go back and read the story as presented in Genesis, you'll discover that one of Joseph's brothers was actually thinking along these lines. His name was Reuben. It was Reuben's idea to throw Joseph in the cistern instead of murdering him immediately. His plan was to quietly rescue Joseph when the brothers were asleep and return him safely to their father. But he wasn't present when the slave traders came by. He missed his opportunity to rescue Joseph. When he discovered his brother had been sold, he tore his clothes in grief.

Here's something I've noticed.

There's usually a Reuben around somewhere.

They are rarely the loudest voice in the room, around the table, or at the bar. But they're around if we'll look for 'em. There's almost always someone who can see our options and inclinations with an eye to our futures. Our stories. Someone who's thinking ultimate rather than immediate. We will come back to that idea later. But for now . . .

Look for Reuben. When you find him, listen to him.

LIKE AN EGYPTIAN

Joseph eventually ends up on an auction block in Egypt where he's purchased by a gentleman named Potiphar. Potiphar was the captain of Pharaoh's palace guard. But now Joseph has a decision to make:

Do I run away?

Do I do what most slaves do, which is as little as possible?

Or do I throw myself into this slave gig with everything I've got?

Interesting dilemma for a rich boy who grew up as the favorite son of his father's favorite wife. A rich boy who no doubt had slaves of his own back home. A rich boy who'd done nothing to deserve this.

Joseph chose door number three and decided to do his best and serve Potiphar's household as if it were his own. Before long, Potiphar notices his second-mile service and gives Joseph more responsibility. The author of Genesis states it this way:

So Potiphar left everything he had in Joseph's care; with Joseph in charge, he did not concern himself with anything except the food he ate.[1]

Thanks to his decision to be all-in, Joseph ends up running Potiphar's entire household. Now that's a story worth telling, isn't it?

---

1. Genesis 39:6.

> I was kidnapped and sold into slavery. I was a victim, but I decided not to live like a victim. I decided to trust God and do the best I could with what I had.

That was the story Joseph opted for.

But then Joseph's story intersected with somebody else's story.

In spite of Joseph's diligence . . . actually, because of his diligence . . . he finds himself in a no-win situation in which he's forced to make yet another decision. This time he's faced with two options, neither of which would lead to a good outcome. The author dribbles out a bit of foreshadowing with the following statement:

> Now Joseph was well-built and handsome . . .

And we can see it coming, can't we?

> . . . and after a while his master's wife took notice of Joseph and said, "Come to bed with me!"[2]

Joseph was probably nineteen or twenty years old by this time. This entire ordeal began when he was just seventeen. He's far from home with no prospects of ever seeing home. It's important to note that for Joseph this was not first and foremost a moral issue. This wasn't primarily about right and wrong. Adultery or fidelity. This was a

---

2. Genesis 39:6–7.

life-or-death issue. He could lose his life either way he chose. He was a slave. He had no rights. Including the right to tell his master's wife no. He didn't have the right to do what was right. But betraying Potiphar wasn't right. Worse. It was dangerous. So he gambled and refused to give in. Day after day she begged him for sex. Day after day he refused.

REHEARSING THE FUTURE

During one of his encounters with Potiphar's wife, Joseph employed a powerful technique. This is one of the primary reasons I chose to illustrate this chapter's question with this account. According to the author, Joseph rehearsed his story out loud as the context for this decision to refuse Potiphar's wife's offer. Somehow, he avoided the trap of allowing this unfortunate situation to overshadow or cause him to lose sight of the broader story of his life. Instead, he views his decision within the context of his story. This is such a powerful idea. Even more amazing, Joseph does this out loud with Potiphar's wife standing there.

Allow me to paraphrase.

"Mrs. Potiphar, I came to this land as a slave. I had no rights and no future. Your husband purchased me. He treated me with kindness. I did my best to serve him and his family as if it were my own. I've worked hard. I've done everything required of me. With my God's help, I've worked my way to the point where your husband trusts me. With everything. He's put me in charge of his entire household."

Then he says, and I quote . . .

"With me in charge . . . my master does not concern himself with anything in the house; everything he owns he has entrusted to my care. No one is greater in this house than I am. My master has withheld nothing from me except you, because you are his wife."[3]

Implication, Mrs. Potiphar, that's your story! You really need to think about this. Do you really want "Affair with a Hebrew slave" on your résumé? Are you sure you want that as part of your story? Then he asks an extraordinary question. In light of all that's happened. In light of your husband's confidence in me and God's mercy to me . . .

"How then could I do such a wicked thing and sin against God?"[4]

In other words, why would I want to add *adultery* and *betrayal* to what's turning out to be a good story with an ending I never dreamed possible? Think about it, Mrs. Potiphar, which story would I rather tell?

---

3. Genesis 39:8–9.
4. Genesis 39:9.

Story #1: Your husband gave me an opportunity I never dreamed would come my way, so I was faithful to him and the God who's been watching out for me.

Or,

Story #2: Your husband gave me an opportunity I never dreamed would come my way, so I took advantage of his trust and had an affair with his wife, dishonoring both him and my God.

The narrator continues:

And though she spoke to Joseph day after day, he refused to go to bed with her or even be with her.[5]

Joseph knew his decision, whichever way he decided, would be a permanent part of his story. So he chose not to give in to her request. But this was humiliating to Potiphar's wife. So, she accused him of trying to rape her. Potiphar had no choice then but to respond to his wife's accusation by punishing Joseph. That he didn't have Joseph executed implies he probably didn't believe his wife. But his hands were tied. So he had Joseph thrown into the prison where political prisoners were kept.

Not a great ending to that chapter in Joseph's story.

---

5. Genesis 39:10.

In spite of this setback, the author assures us: "the LORD was with [Joseph]."[6]

Which is a bit strange.

If the Lord was *with* Joseph, it would seem the Lord would have kept all this from happening to Joseph in the first place. Isn't that what the Lord does? If the Lord was with Joseph, he would've been home with his dad and his dad's favorite wife while his murderous brothers were serving time in Egypt. Right? If the Lord was with Joseph, Potiphar's scheming, no-good wife would have been tossed out, and Joseph would have been rewarded for his integrity. Don't good things come to good people?

Everything about this seems wrong.

But Joseph's story wasn't over.

And regardless of what you're going through right now, your story isn't over either.

It's still being written.

Just like Joseph's.

One decision at a time.

THE EYES OF THE WARDEN

When Joseph gets to prison, he takes a page out of his Life-With-Potiphar playbook.

He gets busy.

He did what was asked plus what he saw needed to be done. Before long he was voted most popular incarceree by

---

6. Genesis 39:21.

the prison warden. Which is not really something you want on a résumé. Besides, if the Lord is with you, you shouldn't know or be known by a prison warden. Not professionally anyway. Eventually the warden turned most of his administrative duties over to Joseph. He was pretty much running the place. But this was the last place Joseph wanted to be.

But it was where he would remain.

For eight long years.

You may know how Joseph's story turned out, but he didn't. For all he knew, prison was all he would ever know. Yet somehow, decision by decision, he just kept writing his story. A good story. A story he doubted anyone would ever hear, much less tell. Certainly not read. No one would go to the expense or trouble to document the story of a Hebrew boy sold into slavery by his brothers. Such measures were reserved for the stories of the Pharaohs.

Eight years into his prison chapter, Joseph was given charge over two new inmates—both former employees of none other than Pharaoh himself—his baker and his cupbearer. Not too long after their incarceration, both gentlemen had dreams they were convinced had significance. But neither was able to make sense of the details of their dreams. During breakfast, Joseph noticed the concerned looks on their faces and expressed his concern. They told him about their dreams and their confusion regarding their meaning. Joseph assured them that the interpretation of dreams belonged to his God and, with their permission and cooperation, he would be happy to see if he could make sense of things.

The cupbearer went first.

When he finished recounting what he remembered of his dream, Joseph smiled and said:

> "Within three days Pharaoh will lift up your head and restore you to your position, and you will put Pharaoh's cup in his hand, just as you used to do when you were his cupbearer."[7]

But what Joseph said next is one of my favorite parts of his story. What he said next reminds us that he was human. Sure, God was with him, but he was ready for God to be with him somewhere else! So he says to the cupbearer:

> "But when all goes well with you, remember me and show me kindness; mention me to Pharaoh and get me out of this prison!"[8]

Then he rehearses a bit of his story.

> "I was forcibly carried off from the land of the Hebrews, and even here I have done nothing to deserve being put in a dungeon."[9]

Joseph was making the best decisions possible under the circumstances. But he was neither happy nor content with the circumstances.

---

7. Genesis 40:13.
8. Genesis 40:14.
9. Genesis 40:13–15.

After hearing Joseph's favorable interpretation of the cup-bearer's dream, the baker was anxious to share his. When he wrapped up, I imagine Joseph was tempted to say, "That's a tough one. I have no idea what your dream means."

But he didn't.

"This is what it means," Joseph said. "Within three days Pharaoh will lift off your head and impale your body on a pole. And the birds will eat away your flesh."[10]

To which the baker probably thought, *Should have kept my dream to myself.*

Sure enough, just as Joseph predicted, three days later Pharaoh celebrated his birthday by having the cupbearer restored and the baker impaled. When Pharoah's guard showed up with orders to release the cupbearer, I imagine Joseph started packing. Surely, out of gratitude, the cup-bearer would grant Joseph's request. Surely it would only be a matter of days, maybe hours, before he was released. But it was not to be. What follows are perhaps the saddest eleven words in the English version of the Hebrew Bible. The author writes:

The chief cupbearer, however, did not remember Joseph; he forgot him.[11]

---

10. Genesis 40:18–19.
11. Genesis 40:23.

It's hard to decide a good story when you've been forgotten, isn't it?

When it feels like nothing we do matters, it's difficult to be concerned about what we do. When we couldn't care less because nobody else cares, we get careless. We make bad decisions. We create regret. Regret never makes for a good story.

A NEW CHAPTER

Two more years crept by.

Joseph had no doubt resigned himself to the fact that finding favor in the eyes of the prison warden was all the favor he would ever find. This was as good as it would get.

And then, everything changed.

Pharaoh had a dream.

Two actually.

Two disturbing dreams.

The author tells us:

In the morning his mind was troubled, so he sent for all the magicians and wise men of Egypt. Pharaoh told them his dreams, but no one could interpret them for him.[12]

And guess who finally spoke up?

Yep, the cupbearer. In all likelihood, the cupbearer

---

12. Genesis 41:8.

spoke up in an attempt to save the day. When you saved Pharaoh's day, there was usually a reward involved. The cupbearer gently reminded Pharaoh of their falling out two years earlier. He went on to describe his encounter with a certain young Hebrew. When he finished with his tale, Pharaoh immediately called for Joseph. After a quick shave and a haircut, Joseph was ushered into the presence of the most powerful man on the planet.

Pharaoh wasted no time relaying his dreams to Joseph. Joseph wasted no time in his response:

"God has revealed to Pharaoh what he is about to do."[13]

To make a long interpretation short, Egypt was going to experience their version of the dot com boom followed immediately by their version of the Great Depression. Only their boom would be way boomier and their depression would be more depressing.

The Egyptian economy was driven by grain prices, which of course was determined by the availability of grain. Because bread was the primary source of food in ancient times, the availability of grain was often the difference between survival and starvation. According to Joseph, Egypt was about to experience seven years of abundant grain production. They would be swimming in grain before it was over. But when it was over, it would be over, over. After seven years of consecutive bumper crops, no one

---

13. Genesis 41:25–26.

would be able to grow a thing. Following the good years there would be a famine in the land, a famine so severe no one would even remember the good years.

Apparently, Joseph's interpretation left everyone in the throne room speechless because Joseph kept right on talking. Having wrapped up his dream interpretation assignment, Joseph did the unthinkable and began giving Pharaoh advice about how to prepare for the coming famine. This included Pharaoh finding someone he trusted and putting that person in charge of grain collection during the good years so the nation would be prepared for the not-so-good years.

Pharaoh's response?

> The plan seemed good to Pharaoh and to all his offi-
> cials. So Pharaoh asked them, "Can we find anyone
> like this man, one in whom is the spirit of God?"[14]

Pharaoh saw in Joseph a man he could trust. Potiphar would vouch for him. The prison warden would vouch for him. The cupbearer had already vouched for him. His reputation was spotless. His track record was impeccable. He had nothing to hide. Nothing to be ashamed of. Before the day was over, Pharaoh appointed Joseph as prime minister of Egypt. His primary responsibility was to store enough grain to sustain the nation through the coming famine.

Joseph's biographer stops at this point in his account to tell his readers that Joseph was thirty years old when

---

14. Genesis 41:37–38.

he stood before Pharaoh. For thirteen unimaginably long and difficult years, Joseph had been writing his story one decision at a time—a story that paved the way for him to become the second most powerful person in the nation that represented the superpower of that day . . . Egypt.

With his new title and responsibility, Joseph did what Joseph always did.

His best.

For the next seven years, Joseph devoted his attention to developing a network of grain storage facilities throughout Egypt. By the end of the seven years of surplus, Egypt was prepared for what was to come. And come it did. A famine devastated that region of the world. Nothing would grow. Anywhere. The areas surrounding Egypt felt it first. They were caught completely off guard. Eventually, even the Egyptian population ate through their surplus grain and cried out to Pharaoh for relief. In response, Joseph opened the storehouses and began selling grain to Egyptians. Word spread quickly that there was grain to be had in Egypt. Before long, foreigners were pouring over the borders into Egypt to purchase grain.

That's when Joseph's story took an interesting turn, a turn that set him up for the most important and most difficult decision of his life.

FAMILY TIES

When Joseph's aging father got word there was grain for sale down in Egypt, he sent Joseph's brothers packing.

When they arrived in Egypt, it just so happened that they showed up at the grain distribution center Joseph was visiting that day. Joseph recognized them immediately. But they had no clue who he was. To them, he was the second most powerful man in the land. So they responded appropriately.

They bowed down with their faces to the ground.

Imagine that moment.

What transpires next is fascinating. For the sake of time, space, and interest, I'll skip to the concluding episode of Joseph's story. But if you've never read the account of Joseph's initial response to his brothers, it's worth looking up.[15]

But before I get to Joseph's response, let's pause, put ourselves in his expensive sandals for a moment, and imagine how he *felt* like responding. How he would have been *justified* in responding. When he was seventeen years old, these ten grown men *sold* him to strangers with no concern for what would happen to him. They profited off his misery, dread, terror, hopelessness, and separation. Whatever he dreamed up, he would certainly be justified. And he had the power to do unto them whatever and however he pleased.

What do you do when you've got the power and your decisions determine your enemy's destiny?

What do you *decide* in a moment like that?

It depends on the story you want to tell. Joseph's response to his brothers is a reminder that unpleasant circumstances

---

15. See Genesis 42–44.

create unprecedented, eye-popping, attention-getting, decision-making opportunities. When you decide what everybody expects you to decide . . . what they would decide if they were you . . . nobody notices. But when you decide against the norm, the tide, human nature, your story stands out.

The author describes Joseph's reveal as follows:

Joseph could no longer control himself before all his attendants, and he cried out, "Have everyone leave my presence!" So there was no one with Joseph when he made himself known to his brothers.[16]

Joseph said to his brothers, "I am Joseph!"[17]

He could have added:

. . . and they wetteth themselves.

Imagine the thoughts that flooded their minds. Joseph's biographer says,

. . . they were terrified at his presence.[18]

They were terrified because they assumed Joseph would decide unto them as they had decided unto him. But Joseph wasn't anything like his brothers. Joseph had decided years

---

16. Genesis 45:1.
17. Genesis 45:3.
18. Genesis 45:3.

earlier to live a story worth telling. He had been deciding a good story for thirteen years. He wasn't going to ruin it now with a revenge chapter. They didn't need to be terrified in his presence because in his absence, Joseph lived as if God was present. So in addition to rescuing the nation from a devastating famine, Joseph rescued his brothers and their families. He moved them all to Egypt, where they settled permanently as guests and relatives of the prime minister.

Good decision.

Good story.

That's why we're still telling it. Revenge stories? There are plenty of those. It's what we expect. It's when we decide against the grain that we decide a story worth repeating.

Before we leave Joseph's story, let's consider for a moment the contrast between Joseph and his brothers. His brothers decided a story they spent their lives hiding. A story that made them liars for life. Joseph had a story he was proud to tell.

Like Joseph, like his brothers, you and I are writing our stories one decision at a time, one day at a time.

Think about that.

You're writing the story that is your life, every day, one decision at a time. If you don't take anything else away from Joseph's story, I hope you'll take this away: Don't ever make a decision that will make you a liar for life. Long after whatever you gained is gone, you'll be left with your lie. You'll be left with a story you won't be proud to tell.

What story do you want to tell?

STILL TELLING IT

I have a close friend who went through a painful and drawn-out divorce proceeding several years ago. His wife was unfaithful. Initially she abandoned my friend and their two children to move in with her boyfriend. Nothing was beneath her when it came to getting what she wanted. Eventually, she recognized the kids were her best leverage and suddenly she was all about the kids.

Jimmy was hurt. But he was angry as well. Especially when his wife began to manipulate the kids to get what she wanted. Throughout the process she lied about her affair, trashed his reputation, and ate up tens of thousands of dollars in unnecessary court costs and attorney's fees.

Early on, in what would turn out to be a two-and-a-half-year court battle, Jimmy and I had dinner. Basically, I told him what I've told you:

> Believe it or not, one day, this entire ordeal will be nothing more than a story you tell. One day, it will be in the rearview mirror of your life. It'll be just one more story; a painful story, but just a story.

And then I asked him what I'm asking you. "Jimmy," I said,

> "What story do you want to tell? What story do you want to tell your kids when they're old enough to understand and begin asking tough questions? When

they want to know the details about what happened between you and their mom? What story do you want to tell? Every decision you make, every critical remark you let slip, becomes part of your story."

I warned him . . .

"You're going to be tempted to be critical of your wife to the kids. You are going to be tempted to look for ways to hurt her the way she's hurt you. You've just got to remember that every decision you make becomes a permanent part of your story."

He teared up.
I teared up.
He nodded. "I want to write a story worth telling."
And he did. And he continues to.
Every few weeks for months, he would call and leave me a voicemail or text me saying, "Andy, I can still tell my whole story." If you had an opportunity to chat with Jimmy, he would look you in the eye and tell you that regardless of what you're going through, one day, it will simply be a story that you tell. Then he would tell you what I've told you, "Write a story you want to tell. And remember, you do that one day, one decision at a time."

Every decision you make becomes part of the story of your life. Every relational, financial, and professional decision and the outcomes of those decisions become permanent parts of your story. We've all lived long enough to have a few chapters we wish we could erase. No doubt you have a few stories you wish you could rewrite. We all do. We call it regret. But chances are, the decisions that led to your greatest regrets could have been avoided if you had paused to ask yourself, "What story do I want to tell?"

From here on out, write a story worth telling. Write a story you're proud to tell. If you're in the middle of making a decision right now, stop and ask yourself: Of the available options, which one do I want as a permanent part of the story of my life?

In chapter two I challenged you to decide to be honest with yourself. As we conclude this chapter, I want to challenge you with a second decision.

Decision #2: The Legacy Decision
I will decide a story I'm proud to tell.
I will not decide anything that
makes me a liar for life.

Every decision you make becomes a permanent part of your story. The story of your life.

What story do *you* want to tell?

What story do you want told *about* you?

The good news is, you get to decide. But you decide one decision at a time, because you write the story of your life . . . one decision at a time.

Write a good one!

— 4 —

The Conscience Question

Is There a Tension That
Deserves My Attention?

I thought it might be fun to begin this chapter with a question that has absolutely nothing to do with you.

Why are people who've had too much to
drink inclined to make bad decisions?

I see that hand.

"Because they've had too much to drink?"

Nope.

Anyone else?

Think about it.

You've heard the stories. Perhaps you *have* some stories. Some funny. Some tragic. Some . . . that are still a bit hazy.

So what is the correlation between alcohol consumption and poor decision-making? To my knowledge, there is no correlation between alcohol and *good* decision-making.

I've never heard a story that concluded with, "So it's a good thing I was drunk. Otherwise, I might have made a really bad decision . . . ."

Back to my *really bad* question:

> Why are people who've had too much to
> drink inclined to make bad decisions?

Physiologically speaking, there are two reasons. Alcohol increases norepinephrine in the brain. Increased norepinephrine acts as a stimulant. Stimulants increase impulsiveness and decrease inhibition. The result is decreased sensitivity to the potential consequences associated with a decision.

Perhaps worse, alcohol temporarily impairs the activity of the prefrontal cortex. This is the part of your brain that enables you to connect the dots. To think rationally. To make good decisions. It's that part of your brain that didn't begin working properly until you were twenty. Or twenty-one. In my case. . . . well, that's another story.

Anyway.

Alcohol liberates a drinker to act without thinking clearly or feeling appropriately. It makes 'em brave when they should be cautious. Loud when they should be quiet. Ron White illustrated it perfectly when he described what followed his being arrested for public drunkenness:

> I had the *right* to remain silent.
> But I did not have the *ability* to.

People who've had too much to drink are inclined to make bad decisions because they are temporarily desensitized to social, cultural, and relational cues. They are chemically impeded from rational thought. They ignore the obvious because it isn't obvious.

To them.

So, inebriated people can't help themselves—once they're inebriated.

When someone is drunk, they don't *consciously* ignore common sense. It's not there to be ignored. They don't *consciously* ignore their conscience. It's been suppressed, switched off. That's why the following afternoon they . . . you? . . . are texting with a friend:

"I did what?"

"Are you sure? I would never . . ."

"There's a video?"

And what does this have to do with you?

Well, if you're drunk, it should be obvious. But of course it isn't. Covered that.

If you're not, here's my point.

Inebriated people *can't* pay attention to the cues around them or the internal tension within them. But we sober people are often guilty of *choosing* to ignore the cues *around* us and the internal tension *within* us. Intoxicated people can't pay attention to social, cultural, and relational cues. But we've all seen sober people refuse to pay attention to those same cues. The inebriated aren't even conscious of their consciences. But we've all seen what happens when sober people choose to ignore their consciences—that internal tension that always deserves our attention.

Intoxicated people *can't* help themselves.

But sober people often *won't* help themselves.

And that leads us to the third question we should pause to ask every time we are making even moderately important decisions.

Question #3: The Conscience Question

Is there a *tension* that deserves my *attention*?

PAYING ATTENTION

Sometimes . . . in fact, more times than we would like to admit . . . an option we're considering creates a little tension inside of us. Something about it is just a bit uncomfortable. Something about it doesn't seem exactly right. It gives us pause. It bothers us. It causes us to hesitate. And oftentimes, we have no idea why.

Experts sometimes refer to this phenomenon as a *red flag moment*, an internal sense of "I'm not sure why, but something about this doesn't feel right." When that happens, you owe it to yourself to pause and pay attention to the tension.

Don't ignore it.

Don't brush it off.

Pause and ask yourself, "What about this bothers me?"

This isn't easy to do. It's not easy for all the same reasons we've talked about. Focalism blurs and exaggerates things. Confirmation bias distorts things. Our schedules compress things. Sometimes *we* are in a hurry. Sometimes *somebody else* is in a hurry. The salesman is always in a hurry. To complicate things further, in most instances we are left with the impression that we are the only ones ill at ease. We look around and nobody else seems to be bothered. Nobody else appears to be wrestling with their conscience. As Joshua Nash warns, it's generally a mistake to take our cues from what does and doesn't bother everybody else when something is bothering us:

> Because of the pressure to fit in and to please, we can find ourselves making decisions that don't align with our highest good. When we make decisions from the fear of being judged and/or rejected, we doom ourselves to this people-pleasing brand of decision-making.[1]

All of this makes it difficult to pause and pay attention to the tension.

Intoxicated people can't.

We can.

We should.

To be clear, I'm not suggesting you prioritize emotion over reason in the decision-making process. But I am suggesting you pay attention to what initially may appear to be an unreasonable emotion. Emotions play an important

---

1. Joshua Nash, LPC-S, *3 Red Flags You're About to Make a Decision You'll Regret*, GoodTherapy.org, April 11, 2016.

role in good decision-making. As Paul Naeger reminds us in his excellent article *Red Flag Decision Making*,

> Emotions serve a purpose, informing us what to do. If our brain comes across something and categorizes it as a "red flag," we will be notified through thoughts and feelings created by emotion. This "red flag" alerts us to pay attention. Our emotions act as a cueing system notifying us to pay attention and take action.[2]

These "red flag" moments are actually a specific part of our brain alerting us to pay attention. And when we pause, we stand a better chance of making a good decision.

So pay attention to the tension.

PAY ATTENTION TO YOUR MOMMA

There's a second, less subtle version of this same phenomenon. I bet this has happened to you a time or two. You're considering something . . . nothing about it bothers you . . . and then somebody comes along and points out something you hadn't thought about. Something you hadn't seen. Suddenly, where there was no tension, there's tension. Where there was no hesitation, you find yourself second-quessing your original intention. Oftentimes, it's irritating.

Oftentimes, it's your mom.

---

2. Paul Andrew Naeger, "Red Flag" Decision Making, August 4, 2015.

"Honey, that all sounds good except for the fact that it's against the law."

Years ago, Sandra and I purchased a piece of residential property that at the time felt like it was on the outskirts of civilization. Our intention was to sell our current home, rent for a year or two, and then build on the new property. Six months after we closed on it, we started having second thoughts. Every time we drove "out there," we were reminded of how far "out there" it was from family, friends, a grocery store, a drug store . . . pretty much everything. So we decided to sell it, confident we'd made a bad decision by purchasing it to begin with. We were two days away from listing it when my mom called:

"Andy, I've been thinking about your lot. And I felt like I was supposed to tell you that I think you'll regret selling it."

"I *felt like* I was supposed to tell you . . ."

What did that even mean? She *felt* like? What did my mom's *feelings* have to do with it? Or anything for that matter.

My mom was in her late sixties at the time. She'd visited the property once. She'd never been in the real estate business. In fact, she'd never been in any business. And, it really wasn't any *of* her business. But of course I was polite. I thanked her for her concern. When I got off the phone, I told Sandra about our conversation. Our short conversation. We both appreciated her concern. We were grateful she felt the freedom to tell us what she was feeling. But ". . . felt like I should tell you . . ." wasn't a reason to reverse our decision.

But we did.

And I'm so glad we did.

That was twenty-one years ago. We've been living on that piece of property for the past nineteen years. It's where we raised our children. If we had sold it, we would have regretted it for the rest of our lives. Civilization caught up and property values did as well. But here's the odd thing. Neither Sandra nor I can remember exactly what it was about my mom's phone call that changed our minds. Our minds were made up. My mom didn't add any new information or insight to the process. What her call added was doubt. Tension. And for reasons I still don't understand to this day, we knew . . . we just knew . . . we needed to pay attention to that tension. As a result, we concluded she was right. Why? I still don't know. But we just knew.

Is there a tension that deserves your attention?

Time for one more?

During my final semester of college, I was trying to decide between three graduate school options. I had been accepted to two but didn't bother to apply to the third because the program was more demanding, a year longer, and thus more expensive. Eventually I settled on a school in Chicago. Sent a deposit. Reserved a dorm and that was that.

Or so I thought.

Then my dad called. "Andy," he said, "I was praying

this morning that God would give you wisdom about where you go to school this fall. I know he will. Just wanted to encourage you."

Encourage me?

For some reason, his *encouragement* actually made me mad.

I didn't tell him I was mad. I thanked him. He was out of town, so we didn't talk long. But when I hung up the phone (something we used to do with phones in the dark ages), I was so frustrated. He knew I'd already chosen a school. He knew I'd sent my deposit and had a roommate. He called to "encourage" me, but I wasn't encouraged—I was mad! And that didn't make sense. Why would I be angry about my dad praying for me and calling me to tell me he was praying for me? He wasn't the passive-aggressive type. If he'd disagreed with my choice of schools, he would have told me straight up.

But there it was.

That tension.

I had my mind made up, but now I was all churned up.

As a result of that short, but oh-so-disruptive conversation, I applied to and attended the school with the longer, more rigorous program. My unreasonable response to my dad's call eventually led me to realize . . . harking back to our first question . . . that I hadn't been honest with myself. I hadn't been honest with myself about why I hadn't bothered to apply to the third school. Truth was, I was afraid. I was afraid I wouldn't get in and, even if I did, I wouldn't be able to do the work.

What did my dad's call have to do with any of that? Nothing.

But it created a tension. A tension that deserved my attention. And I'm so glad I paid attention.

Is there a tension that deserves your attention?

FRIENDS DON'T LET FRIENDS

But it's not just our parents. Sometimes it's a friend.

"Sounds good to me, but what's your wife going to think when she finds out?"

Tension.

"Can you afford that?"

Tension.

"Didn't you sign a noncompete?"

Tension.

"I thought you were on a diet?"

Meddling.

The problem with someone else bringing things to our attention is that it creates relational tension. And that's a tension you should pay attention to as well. Why? Because we have a tendency to discount *truth* by discounting the *truth bearer.* Seriously, what does your roommate know? He's not any further along in life than you are. Your sister-in-law? She can't even run her own life. Your neighbor? What does he know about parenting? His kids are so young. In philosophy, there's actually a name for this dynamic. It's called the *genetic fallacy* or the *fallacy of origins.* We fall prey to this fallacy when we discount information based on the *source* rather than the *merits* of the information. What did my mom know about residential real estate?

Nothing.

But she was still right.

So pay attention to the tension regardless of the source. Besides, you've given plenty of people plenty of good advice you didn't take yourself, right? But you were still right, right?

LET IT BE

As you consider your options, as you consider moving down a particular path, as you consider what to do next, if there's *any* hesitation around a particular alternative, pause and allow . . . and I don't know any other way to say this . . . allow that emotion, that tension, to rise up and get as big as it can possibly get before you decide. Don't start selling yourself. As we've discussed, we have the ability to sell ourselves right past that pesky tension that deserves our attention.

If something bothers you, let it bother you. If something bothers you about him . . . about her . . . about that job . . . that offer . . . that invitation . . . that deal . . . that contract . . . face it. Embrace it. Don't excuse it. Face that tension until either it goes away or you decide to go a different way. Pay attention to the tension. What begins as an uneasy *feeling* is often supported later with reason. Information. Insight. But if you don't pause, you won't see it.

WHEN SECONDS COUNT

There is a fascinating piece of narrative in the Old Testament that both illustrates and illuminates this dynamic. I say *illuminates* because, as we are about to discover, this story parallels circumstances you will experience some day, if you haven't already.

The story revolves around King David, Israel's second king, long before he became king. As you may know, David steps onto the pages of history as a boy shepherd. When he was a kid, a prophet showed up at his home and announced to his family that God had chosen David to be the next king of Israel.

That's a good day.

When one of your children is chosen to be the next king . . . good day.

Problem was, Israel already had a king. King Saul. But Saul wasn't doing a very good job kinging. So, according to the prophet Samuel, God had decided to replace him. But not with Saul's son, as was customary. God decided to make a dynasty change. So he sent the prophet to the house of Jesse to anoint David king. Then David's father sent David back out into the countryside to tend sheep.

In time, David became a soldier in King Saul's army. Before long, his popularity overshadowed that of King Saul. Saul becomes jealous and tries to kill David. David fled the city and becames a fugitive. But by now David had become a legend. The incident with Goliath when he was younger established his reputation as a warrior and leader.

Consequently, dozens and then hundreds of fugitives and outlaws flocked to David's side. Soon he had a small army of his own. But an army without a home. An army made up primarily of men who, like David, were on the run from the law. And that's where we'll pick up the story as told to us by the prophet Samuel.

> After Saul returned from pursuing the Philistines, he was told, "David is in the Desert of En Gedi." So Saul took three thousand able young men from all Israel and he set out to look for David and his men. . . . He came to the sheep pens along the way; a cave was there, and Saul went in to relieve himself.[3]

Get the picture?

Saul and three thousand soldiers are trekking through the wilderness looking for David. They know he and his merry men are in the vicinity. And speaking of the vicinity, if you visit Jerusalem, you can actually drive to En Gedi and see the area where David hid from Saul. It's rocky, barren desert for hundreds and hundreds of miles. And all along the sides of the mountains are caves. Thousands of caves.

Back to the story.

In the middle of his search for David, nature calls. King Saul has to go to the bathroom. Whereas everybody else in Saul's caravan would just have to deal with it, when you're

---

3. 1 Samuel 24:1–3.

king, you can stop the parade to go take care of business. But, when you're king, you don't relieve yourself in public. So Saul gives the signal for all three thousand men plus the caravan of donkeys, mules, camp followers, and pack animals to come to a halt. Then he heads up into the hills to find a suitable place to relieve himself. And what would serve the purpose better than a dark cool cave? And this is where the story takes an interesting twist.

David and his men were far back in the cave.[4]

As in the very cave Saul randomly chose. What are the odds of that? Talk about the stars lining up . . . the gods smiling on you. From David's perspective, this was a best-case scenario.

Apparently, when David got word that Saul and his oversized posse were headed his way, he told his men to scatter to the surrounding hills until Saul and company passed through. At which point, David and his men would regather and escape in the opposite direction. And everything was working according to plan until Saul gets nature's call, dismounts his mule, and hikes up to the very cave where David and a handful of his men were hiding. When they realized he was headed in their direction, they moved farther into the darkness.

By the time Saul appears as a silhouette in the mouth of the cave, David's eyes have adjusted to the darkness. Saul,

---

4. 1 Samuel 24:3.

on the other hand, had just stepped in from the bright Middle-Eastern sun. He can't see anything. He moves in just far enough to ensure his privacy, takes off his robe, throws it to the side, hikes up his outer garment, squats down, and opens a magazine.

Well, he squatted down.

What do you think is running through David's mind?

What would be running through your mind if you were in David's predicament?

Clearly this was an omen. A sign from God. God had delivered his enemy into his hand. What else could it mean? He'd already been anointed king. Everybody in Israel knew he was next. The only thing standing in his way was the current king. And here he is, unguarded and about as vulnerable as a king can get. If David wasn't thinking that way, we know his men were because of what happens next:

> The men said, "This is the day the LORD spoke of when he said to you, 'I will give your enemy into your hands for you to deal with as you wish.'"[5]

This was exactly what David promised his men would happen. As they sat around a fire at night, away from their families, unable to go home because of the prices on their heads, David had assured them that it wouldn't be this way forever. Eventually, he assured them, he would take his rightful place as king, and when he did, those who

---

5. 1 Samuel 24:4.

had been loyal to him in the lean years would be rewarded handsomely.

Now the waiting was over!

Decision made.

Kill the king and go home.

Imagine the optics. Three thousand soldiers watch as Saul enters the cave. Then, to their utter amazement, they see David step out of the cave with Saul's severed head hoisted by his hair. Saul's men would immediately proclaim David king. No civil war. No bloodshed. Well, minimal bloodshed. Thousands of lives would be spared. It was perfect. Again, there was no decision to be made. It was a matter of "kill the king before he kills you!" Besides, what other options were there? Remain outlaws for the rest of their lives? This needed to end, and now was the perfect time to end it.

Imagine the emotion in the cave that afternoon. The adrenaline. Imagine the pressure David felt to act, to save his men from another season of hiding out like bandits and risking their lives day after day. But David felt something else as well. A tension. A hesitation. Something wasn't exactly right about all of this. But that inner hesitation made no sense in light of the circumstances in which he and his loyal men found themselves.

So he decided to act anyway.

Then David crept up unnoticed . . .[6]

---

6. 1 Samuel 24:4.

David takes his dagger and creeps up behind Saul with every intention of ending his life. His men are watching from the recesses. If David is successful, the world as they know it would change instantly. But as David gets closer, the tension intensifies. In spite of the fact that there seemed to be no alternative, David paid attention to that tension. He paused long enough to allow what was bothering him to really bother him. And somewhere between leaving his hiding place in the back of the cave and Saul's unprotected back, it dawns on him. Literally, just a few feet away, seconds away, from a decision that everybody would applaud, he gains clarity around the tension that had captured his attention.

He was about to murder the king!

That couldn't be right.

Besides, David was all too aware of *who* chose Saul to be king to begin with.

The same God, who through the same prophet, had chosen him to be king as a kid. Who was he to replace the man God had put in place? It wasn't his place to kill the king even if the king was trying to kill him. In spite of unimaginable pressure to act, in spite of the expectations of those around him, David changes course.

Back to the story in a moment.

We all have something in common with David at this point in the narrative. David didn't know what the outcome of his decision to kill Saul would be. There was no guarantee things would work out as he envisioned them working out. Right? He thought he knew. His men thought they knew. Kill the king, become the king. Problem solved. Right? But there was no guarantee that would be the outcome.

Please don't miss this.

One of the reasons we ignore the tension when we are making decisions . . . one reason we push through and ignore the advice of other people or the voice of our conscience is: *We believe we can predict outcomes.* Don't we? We think we know. But we don't know. You don't always predict outcomes accurately, do you? Does anybody? If you've ever been disappointed, you know this to be the case.

What is disappointment?

Disappointment is always connected to an unexpected outcome. When you make a decision assuming an outcome and the outcome doesn't materialize, what do you experience? Disappointment. Ignoring that tension in your gut sets you up for disappointment. Paying attention to that tension is how you avoid unnecessary disappointment.

Back to David.

Just a few feet away from Saul, it occurs to David: Just because I kill the king doesn't mean I will necessarily become king. But one thing is for certain . . . I will be the man who killed the king! That will be my legacy. That will be the story I'll be forced to tell my children and grandchildren. "Grandpa David, tell us one more time about how you became king. You know, how you snuck up behind King Saul while he was using the potty and slit his throat!"

The author tells us David was *conscience-stricken.*

His conscience bothered him for even considering the deed he almost carried out. This is how we know he was paying attention to the tension. He was paying attention to his conscience.

What happens next is remarkable. David does something very few people have the self-control to do. He changed course mid-stream. Instead of murdering Saul, he creeps up behind him and cuts off a corner of his discarded robe. Then he makes his way back to his hiding place where his men are staring in utter disbelief. They were so close to going home only to watch the opportunity slip away. The expressions on their faces said it all. David had some explaining to do.

> He said to his men, "The LORD forbid that I should do such a thing to my master, the LORD's anointed . . ."

To which his men must have thought, *Well then, let one of us do it!* David continued:

> "The LORD forbid that I should do such a thing to my master, the LORD's anointed, or lay my hand on him; for he is the anointed of the LORD." With these words David sharply rebuked his men and did not allow them to attack Saul. And Saul left the cave and went his way.[7]

---

7. 1 Samuel 24:6–7.

Saul exits the cave, having no clue as to how close he came to joining his dead ancestors. Instead, he rejoins his men. He climbs back up on his mule and is preparing to continue his search for David when suddenly he hears a voice coming from the direction he just departed. The text tells us David stepped out of the mouth of the cave and began to call to the king.

"Saul, Saul."

Talk about drama. Three thousand men hear a voice, they look, and there stands the very man they've been hunting. The man they were paid to kill. There stands David in the mouth of the cave King Saul just exited.

The text says David bowed down to Saul from the mouth of the cave. Then he stands to his feet, holds up the corner of Saul's garment and announces to all present that he could have easily murdered the king but chose not to. For all who were gathered that day, one thing was clear: David was the better man. He spared Saul's life when Saul would have taken his.

After a short speech, David concludes with this powerful, powerful statement—a statement that we should all take to heart:

"May the LORD judge between you and me . . ."

In other words, "Saul, I'm going to do the right thing. The just thing. I will wait and allow God to determine

the outcome of this conflict. While this may be the worst
political, military, and leadership decision I've ever made,
while I realize I may have just forfeited my life by allowing
you to walk out of here alive, I will not take matters into
my own hands. God made you king. I will not replace what
God put in place. I'll leave that to God. I will not play God
in your life or mine. He continued:

> ". . . may the LORD avenge the wrongs you have done
> to me, but my hand will not touch you."[8]

David wisely decided not to use Saul's bad behavior
as an excuse to do bad things. He would not become like
his enemy.

> "May the LORD be our judge and decide between
> us. May he consider my cause and uphold it; may he
> vindicate me by delivering me from your hand."[9]

Amazing.

Paying attention to that unexplainable, seemingly irra-
tional tension is important for all of us. But for those of us
who believe in a personal God, a God who genuinely cares
for us . . . this is extraordinarily important.

Here's why.

That internal hesitation, that red flag, is often God's
way of turning us in another direction. People yielded to

---

8. 1 Samuel 24:12.
9. 1 Samuel 24:15.

God don't attempt to play God. They don't predict outcomes. Instead, they surrender. They obey. They follow. As much as they want anything, they want to be able to lie in bed at night knowing that things are good between them and their heavenly Father. And rightly so. As my dad is fond of saying: "God takes full responsibility for the life wholly yielded to him."

So pay attention to the tension. If you don't, you may wake up on the other side of a decision you wish you could go back and unmake.

That was certainly the case with Saul.

There he stands, all eyes on him. Humiliated by David. Not by David's military skill. Humiliated by David's humility. His character. His sensitivity to his own conscience. So what do you do in a situation like that if you're Saul? Continue the pursuit? Pursue a man who could have taken your life but chose not to? Even Saul knew better. So he turned his army around and headed back to Jerusalem.

UNEXPECTED ENDING

Not long after his humiliating encounter with David, King Saul and his army find themselves embroiled in a battle with the Philistines. As the day wore on, a random Philistine archer, stationed just behind his infantry, launched an arrow into the sky to fall randomly among the Israelite army. But this random archer's random arrow found a seam in Saul's armor and mortally wounded him. Saul doesn't want to die at the hand of his enemy, so he falls on his own sword and dies as the Israelite army is routed.

When word reaches the city, the citizens lose no time in proclaiming David king. He becomes king without having to murder a king. Perhaps David thought to himself: *Well, if somebody had told me it was going to work out like this, it certainly would have made that whole cave episode a lot easier.*

If God had shown up and said, "Hang on, David, seven chapters from now the Philistines are gonna take care of Saul for you. Relax," it would have certainly made things easier. But that's not how life works, is it? That's why we have to pay attention to the tension. That's why we dare not take matters into our own hands. That's why we dare not trust our ability to predict the future. Outcomes. That's why you must ask yourself, "Is there a *tension* that deserves my attention?"

SCHOOL DAYS

Several years ago, I was helping my daughter, Allie, prepare for an exam. She was in the eighth grade at the time. As we were navigating our way through her study guide, it occurred to me that Garrett, her older brother, had the same teacher in the same class two years prior. I suggested we search Garrett's room for an old test to study from . . . like you do in college.

Right?

Sort of right?

We went digging around and sure enough we found an old test. I assured Allie that her teacher changed the tests from semester to semester. Otherwise, he wouldn't have given them back. So we used the test to study from. The next day she went in to take the test and it was the same test!

When she got home that afternoon, I asked her how *we* did on *our* test. "Dad, you're not going to believe what happened," she said. "It was the same test Garrett had." Then she said, "and I felt like I was cheating." At which point I interrupted and said, "No, no, no. That wasn't cheating." Then I went on to give her my convoluted explanation about why using an old test isn't cheating. If he were a good teacher, he would have changed the test. He knows this stuff is floating around. I reminded Allie that she was an A student and that she would have done well regardless. I continued trying to ease her conscience when she finally interrupted me and said: "Dad, it's okay. I told Mr. Simpson what happened."

I'm like, "What? You told on yourself?"

She said, "Yeah, I told him I had a copy of Garrett's old test that I used to study from, and that it was the same test."

Pause.

Isn't that what you would have done in the eighth grade? No? Me neither.

I said, "Allie, I'm so proud of you. And I feel bad for getting you into trouble. What happened?" "Nothing," she said. "He said he had planned to change the test and at the last minute the copy machine wasn't working, so he used an old test and that it wasn't a problem."

Fortunately, this is not a book about parenting.

Allie sensed a tension. She had a decision to make. A decision she didn't anticipate having to make. Do I tell my teacher or not? When she thought about "not," there was a tension. That just didn't seem like the right thing to do in spite of what her daddy told her. So she paid attention to the tension (rather than to her father) and told her teacher the truth. And I'm so glad she did.

Cute story.

So what?

SOMEWHERE BETWEEN

Here's what I know about you. The decision you're wrestling with right now falls somewhere between choosing whether or not to tell your math teacher you studied from an old test and murdering a king.

Right?

But the principle is the same. If there's something in you, something you can't put your finger on, or perhaps something someone else has put a finger on that bothers you about an option you're considering, pause and pay attention. That tension may very well be God's way of protecting you. It may be his way of waving you off from a decision you'll later regret. Every time you make a decision, especially a decision that takes you by surprise, like David's decision, ask yourself, "Is there a tension that deserves my attention?" Don't ignore it. Don't brush by it. Let it bother you until you know why it bothers you.

In chapters one and two, I challenged you to make specific commitments related to each of our first two questions. Here are two additional commitments I highly encourage you to consider:

Decision #3: The Conscience Decision

I will *pause* even when I can't pin-
point the *cause* of my hesitation.
I will *explore*, rather than *ignore* my conscience.

Is there a tension that deserves your attention?
If so, pay attention to that tension.
That's a decision you will never regret.

— 5 —

The Maturity Question

What Is the Wise Thing to Do?

Remember curfew?

Curfew is a terrible idea.

Well . . . the *traditional* approach to curfew is a terrible idea.

At sixteen years old, curfew transformed me into an overly aggressive weekend night driver.

On weekdays, I was fine. But on Friday and Saturday nights? Not so much.

And you already know why.

The end of every date was always divided into several five-minute increments. "Just five more minutes. I can stay for five more minutes." Five minutes later, "I can stay for five more minutes, just five minutes." Before I knew it, I had to be home in . . . you guessed it. Actually, you may remember it. I had to be home in five minutes! I had to be home in five minutes regardless of how many minutes it would take me.

When my boys started driving, I imposed a different version of curfew. I didn't tell 'em what time to be home. I told 'em what time to *leave* for home. Thanks to cell technology, I knew if they left on time.

HUMAN NATURE

You've experienced some version of the curfew dynamic as an adult, where your *margin for error* was gobbled up with *just-five-more-minutes* thinking. Whether it's one more drink, one more bite, one more business trip, one more stack of chips, one more pair of shoes, or one more swipe of the card, the outcome is usually the same.

One more rarely *adds* anything.

It usually subtracts.

One more often results in less of what we value most, which makes no sense. But it doesn't stop us.

While it's been a while since a curfew dictated your driving habits, your current driving habits are, in fact, influenced by a similar dynamic. Unless you're an unusual driver, you drive at speeds *at* or slightly *above* the posted speed limit. While *most* of us feel little to no guilt about driving faster than the posted speed limit, *none* of us want to get pulled over for speeding. So we choose the speed we're convinced allows us to *break* the law while avoiding an encounter *with* the law. And in most cases, no harm done.

The point?

Whether it's curfew, diet, driving, or spending . . . our natural inclination is to live as close to the line as possible.

What line? The line between legal and illegal. The line between responsible and irresponsible. The line between moral-ish and immoral. Ethical and unethical. The line between "I'm still in control" and "I need help." It's human nature to snuggle up to the edge of irresponsibility, disaster, or embarrassment and stay there as long as possible. It's human nature to get by with as much as we can get by with without becoming our own worst enemy, without undermining our own success, without being grounded, expelled, fired, or kicked out of the house.

THE WRONG QUESTION

Fueling our incessant flirtation with disaster is an unexamined assumption that informs our decision-making. Unexamined assumptions are dangerous. We all have 'em. An assumption anchored to reality is helpful. In all likelihood the sun will rise tomorrow, so you should set your alarm. But an assumption anchored to nothing other than our personal experiences is not only unhelpful, it can be dangerous. This is why it's important to bring all our assumptions into the light of day. Doing so removes the sharp edges from our opinions. It reduces prejudice. It expands the frontiers of our compassion and empathy. Eradicating false assumptions from our conscious and subconscious makes us better.

Specifically, it makes us better decision-makers.

It makes us better decision-makers because we aren't misled by erroneous assumptions.

So what is this unexamined assumption that makes us comfortable living, dating, spending, eating, drinking, driving, and flirting so close to the edge of embarrassment or worse? For the sake of clarity and emphasis, I'll state this unexamined and oh-so-flawed assumption four ways:

> If it's not wrong, it's alright.
> If it's not illegal, it's permissible.
> If it's not immoral, it's acceptable.
> If it's not over the line, it's fine.

If the problem with those sorts of assumptions is not immediately apparent, just put on your older brother or sister hat for a moment. If you're a parent, put on your parent hat. I bet you don't set the bar that low for your kids. This is tantamount to organizing our lives around the lowest common denominator. Essentially we're asking, *How low can I go?* How close can I get to bad without being bad? How close can I get to *wrong* without doing something wrong? Or if you're religious, how close can I get to sin without actually sinning?

There's something to shoot for.

But it doesn't stop there.

Before long we're asking, *How far over the line can I go without getting caught or experiencing consequences?* How unethical, immoral, or insensitive can I be without creating unmanageable outcomes? How long can I neglect my family, my finances, or my health without feeling the effects? How much can I indulge an addictive behavior without actually becoming addicted? It's a slippery, sinister slope. And it all begins by asking the wrong question: Is there anything *wrong* with this?

A question that often leads to a second question: How did I get myself *into* this?

Here's another angle.

Why do good parents tell their children to be *careful*?

Why don't we say things like: "Drive as fast as the law allows!" "Drink your limit!" "Go as far as you can without getting slapped!" "Don't come home until curfew."

What do we mean by *careful*?

We mean *use caution*. Be *aware* of your surroundings. Don't take *unnecessary* risks. Don't jeopardize your safety or the safety of others. Essentially what we're saying is *don't dangle your toes off the edge of illegal, immoral, unsafe, or unhealthy.*

That's good advice.

For everybody.

You might have avoided your greatest nonchildhood regret if you had embraced that posture. You'll certainly avoid regret in the future if you do.

One more.

Why do we react immediately when we see a toddler playing at the edge of a swimming pool? They aren't drowning. They aren't even wet.

Well, they aren't wet on the outside.

Why do we panic?

We panic because we know that one small step in the wrong direction could result in tragedy. We panic because there is virtually no margin for error. When we attempt to warn a teenager standing on the brink of tragedy, they say what we say: "I'm fine. I'm not doing anything wrong." And they're right. But we don't rush to the aid of toddlers and we don't speak to the precarious circumstances of teenagers because they're doing anything *wrong*.

Nobody is doing anything *wrong* until they are.

Drawing our lines, setting our limits, establishing our moral and ethical standards on the borderline between right and wrong, legal and illegal, healthy and unhealthy eliminates any margin for error. It's a foolish and dangerous way to live. You're dry and safe and then you're drowning. You're sober and then you're not.

This explains why we respond the way we do when someone we love is snuggling up to that elusive line. We react not to what they are doing but to the direction they are heading. We seemingly overreact because the margin of error is such that one wrong move could spell disaster or regret.

In those moments, the issue is not right or wrong, legal or illegal, moral or immoral. There's *something else* in play. Something that remains virtually invisible to us when it pertains to us. But something as apparent as the nose on our face when it comes to our children, a niece or nephew, or perhaps the child of a close friend.

What is that something?

Wisdom.

An option can be both *not wrong* and *unwise* at the same time. And that brings us to our fourth question. The maturity question.

Question #4: The Maturity Question

What is the wise thing to do?

To avoid the *five-more-minutes* syndrome . . . to create moral, ethical, and financial margin . . . ask of every invitation, opportunity, and option: *What is the wise thing for me to do?* We've never met, but here's something I know about you. Your greatest regret . . .

And I'm talking about that *moment* of regret. The moment you would give anything to go back and relive or undo. The tipping point. The point of no return. Your greatest regret was preceded by a series of unwise decisions. They weren't wrong. They weren't illegal or immoral. But looking back, they were terribly unwise. And it was that series of unwise decisions that paved the way to the moment in time you've regretted ever since.

Right?

How did I know?

It's the way of things.

Because there isn't a "Thou shalt not" attached to it doesn't necessarily mean "Thou shalt." It's foolish to live on the border of what's permissible, legal, acceptable, not prosecutable.

CAREFUL AND CAUTIOUS

Our first three questions were anchored to ancient wisdom and, as it turns out, our fourth question is as well. The apostle Paul, in a letter to Christians living in Ephesus, writes:

Be very careful, then, how you live—not as unwise
but as *wise*, making the most of every opportunity,
because the days are evil.[1]

Two things stand out about Paul's instructions. First,
how relevant his two-thousand-year-old advice is today.
Some things never change. Human nature never changes.
Ancient folks were as prone as we moderns to snuggle up to
disaster and stay there as long as possible. But perhaps the
most remarkable thing about Paul's instruction is what he
doesn't say. Paul was a Pharisee. He had known and taught
the Jewish Torah his entire adult life. Once he became a
Jesus follower, his perspective of the Jewish law changed,
but he didn't abandon the moral, ethical, or relational
guidelines he was raised with. As a Jesus follower, Paul
was well aware that Jesus had actually raised the bar rather
than lowered it. This is what makes his instructions to
Ephesian Christians a bit surprising. We would expect
Paul to anchor his readers' decision-making to something
more specific and concrete than *wisdom*. But he doesn't.
And he tells us why.

And this is important.

He was aware of what each of us has already discovered. The point of regret is always preceded by a series of
unwise decisions. With that in mind . . . with that in the
background of his own life . . . he says:

---

1. Ephesians 5:15–16, emphasis added.

Be very careful how you live.

To state it in the negative, *Don't be careless how you live*. Then he leverages our word:

Not as unwise, but as *wise*.

With those six words, Paul discloses the criterion by which he and we are to weigh our options. This is the grid through which we are to evaluate every invitation and opportunity. This is the standard, the yardstick by which we are to assess our financial, relational, and professional decisions. And thus our question:

What is the wise thing to do?

Paul follows up with a bit of explanation and motivation:

. . . making the most of every opportunity,

Literally, *redeeming* or *ransoming* the *time*. Don't you wish you could go back and somehow *reclaim* all the time you wasted on bad decisions along with the time spent making up for bad decisions? I do. For you that may be a few weeks or weekends scattered about your past. Or it may be an entire season of life. Either way, imagine having the opportunity to re-live, re-spend, or re-allot those days, weeks, or years. What if you had an opportunity to go back and invest that time in productive, healthy, life-giving activities? Imagine where you might be today. Imagine how different things might be. And while we're daydreaming, imagine being able to reclaim and reinvest all the money you wasted during those seasons.

Yeah, sorry to bring that up.

As painful and as awkward as it might be to look back, it's necessary to understand the invitation embedded in Paul's words. Paul's words are an invitation to invest your time wisely going forward. From this moment on, you are invited to make the most of . . . to redeem . . . to leverage your most important asset, your time, in a way that propels you toward a preferred future. That invitation is fueled by wisdom, being careful rather than careless.

Paul offers another bit of motivation to his instruction as well. He warns:

> . . . making the most of every opportunity, *because the days are evil.*

Evil days?
What's he talking about?
We don't live in a morally neutral culture.
Bet you knew that.

ASLEEP AT THE WHEEL

Every day we interface with a culture that encourages us in the most provocative ways imaginable to satisfy appetites that can never be fully and finally satisfied. Long gone are the days when you had to go looking for trouble. Trouble is always just a click away. Right? Again, Paul's words are so relevant. We can't afford to be careless. We don't live in a morally neutral environment. It's not safe out there. Most Americans are overweight and overleveraged. We eat too much and spend too much. American men spend billions of dollars . . . billions . . . every year looking at pictures of women on their computer screens. That's as amazing as it is embarrassing.

Like the Ephesians in Paul's day, we live in morally and ethically perilous times. The days are evil. If we don't pay attention, if we aren't careful, we will end up paying a price for our carelessness. If we aren't intentionally cautious, we may end up unintentionally corralled by a vice we've always condemned. If we don't filter our choices through this powerful question, we will more than likely find ourselves face-to-face with consequences that could have been, and should have been, avoided.

To state it plainly . . .

Our world is a bit like the beautifully manicured grass outside my kitchen door where we let our dog out to do her business every morning and evening. If you're not careful how you walk, you'll step in it. Worse, you'll bring it into the house!

THIS IS YOUR WAKE-UP CALL

I'll be honest. The challenge with the *wisdom* question is that it forces us to face up to the very thing or things we are trying to ignore. It's like an alarm clock for our consciences. A wake-up call for our souls. It's irritating, but necessary. Perhaps it was the universal propensity to wear out our internal snooze buttons that drove the apostle Paul to continue with these words:

Therefore do not be foolish . . .

If punctuation had been available in the first century, this phrase may have come with double exclamation marks. "Do not be foolish" is a polite way of saying, "Don't be a fool! Don't approach life as if you lived in a morally and ethically neutral environment!" From there he commands readers to do something that appears to be impossible.

. . . but understand what the Lord's will is.[2]

You can't command someone to understand something, can you? I had a Greek teacher in college who would have us come up to the front of the room and translate out loud for the class. There I was with my paperback copy of *The Iliad* standing in front of my peers bluffing my way through some incident from the Trojan War and filling in the gaps with my own editorial comments. When it became evident that I was no longer translating but merely telling the story from memory, Mrs. Cuntz would stop me and say, "Mr. Andy, I don't think you are translating. Translate!"

---

2. Ephesians 5:17.

To which I would reply: "Mrs. Cuntz, I can't translate it."

Her reply was always the same. "Yes, you can! Now translate it for us."

"I really can't."

"Yes, you can. Now translate."

She insisted we understood more than we did, as if her insistence would somehow increase our capacity. It didn't. Eventually she would wave us back to our seats. I always felt like Mrs. Cuntz took my lack of understanding personally, like she had failed me as a teacher.

Whenever I read Paul's admonition to "understand what the Lord's will is," I think of Mrs. Cuntz exhorting us to *understand* Plato. You can inspire an athlete to perform better, but you can't inspire someone to understand something. They either understand it or they don't. So what's Paul up to? Why didn't he say, "*Discover* what the will of the Lord is"? Or "*Obey* the will of the Lord"? We could find traction with either of those. But *understand*?

His point?

FACE-OFF

Paul's command to "understand" God's will is an exhortation to *face up to* what we know in our hearts we ought to do. We are masters in the art of self-deception. So Paul, leveraging the grammar of his day, reaches off the page, grabs us by the collar, pulls us up close, and shouts, "Quit playing games! Quit pretending. Quit rationalizing! Face up to what you know you ought to do! Ask the question and embrace the answer!" This is Paul's final attempt to get us to admit what we know and act on it.

As commonsense as all this sounds, truth is, most folks don't make the wise choice until it's their only choice. By then they're attempting to reclaim something they've lost or are about to lose. Like you, I have friends who changed their unhealthy eating habits overnight after a brush with cancer or heart disease. Lumps, clogs, or shortness of breath forces us to face up to what we've refused to acknowledge for years. Revelations such as these often lead to death-defying discipline.

But why do we wait?

To leverage Paul's words, we wait because we are unwilling to *face up to* what we've known all along. When we quit lying to ourselves, it's amazing what happens. Everyone I know who has undergone a transformation following a health scare says the same thing: "I should have made these changes years ago." Translated: "For years I refused to face up to what I knew in my heart was true."

Bankruptcy can have the same effect. So can a surprise pregnancy, a letter from your spouse's attorney, a DUI, or a trip to detox with one of your kids. And perhaps that's what it will take. There is something out there somewhere that has the ability to get your attention, something that will force you to face up! Unfortunately, that something may scar you as well as scare you. You may be left with limited options and reduced opportunities. So why let things go that far? Why not face up now to what you know in your heart you need to do? Why not ask, *What is the wise thing to do?*

REFERENCE POINTS

When I was a kid, we lived in Miami. Every summer we would pull our eighteen-foot travel trailer to Naples, Florida, for a week of vacation. If you've been to Naples lately, you know the waterfront is lined with condos and hotels. But in 1968, there was nothing but miles of empty beach. So my dad would actually pull out onto the beach and drive along the tree line where the sand was firm. We would drive for miles until we found a suitable place to set up camp.

Of course, the whole point of camping on the beach is *the beach*. But before my sister and I were allowed in the water, we would walk with my dad thirty or forty yards down the tree line away from our camper, where he would send us inland to gather up as many coconuts as we could find lying in the brush. When he felt like we'd collected enough, we would help him transport our plunder down to where high tide had left its mark in the sand. Then we would help him build our annual coconut pyramid. When it was complete, we would race back to the camper to put on our swimsuits in preparation for a week of sand and saltwater.

As you may have guessed, the coconuts served as a reference point. The undertow, though not dangerous, was strong enough to slowly move us down the beach away from our camper. As we neared the coconut pile, we knew it was time to come out of the water, walk back up the beach, and reenter the surf in front of our camper . . . or even a few yards beyond it in the other direction.

Like the undertow in Naples, culture has a way of slowly and subtly edging us beyond healthy moral, ethical, financial, and professional limits. Then one day we look up and wonder who moved the camper! Our actual response is more along the lines of, "How did I get myself into this situation?" When everything and everybody is drifting along at the same rate in the same direction, it's easy to be lulled into believing you're standing still. Without a stationary reference point, it's impossible to ascertain where you are, where you aren't, and where you ought to be.

So if you will allow me to be so bold, I would like to suggest you establish three reference points that relate to our fourth question. These will be easy to remember because each of the three is simply an extension of the question. Here they are all rolled into one memorable phrase:

> In light of my *past* experience, my *current*
> circumstances, and my *future* hopes and dreams,
> what is the *wise* thing for me to do?

Let's begin with the past.

YOUR PAST EXPERIENCE

Poet and philosopher George Santayana is credited with the familiar quip, "Those who cannot remember the past are condemned to repeat it." On a personal level, that axiom could be restated this way: "Those who don't pay attention to what got 'em into trouble yesterday are liable to end up in the same trouble tomorrow."

Not as catchy, but you get the point.

Your past predisposes you to specific temptations, addictions, attractions, and blind spots. You're a sucker for . . . something, right? Consequently, what's okay for everybody else may be off-limits for you. What some folks consider a pastime may actually be a pathway to something destructive for you. There are activities others find it easy to walk away from while you are prone to overindulge. So every decision, invitation, and opportunity that comes your way needs to be filtered through this question: In light of *my* past experience, what's the wise thing for *me* to do?

I have a friend (we'll call him Steve) who received some unsettling advice halfway through premarital counseling. His counselor said, "Steve, your family history is such that when you and Shawna return from your honeymoon, you need to come back in to see me. Alone. In fact, when you get back, I would like to introduce you to a counselor who specializes in family systems."

Like most men, Steve felt like he had already gone the extra mile attending (as well as paying for) four hour-long premarital sessions. Now this! Steve's next question was the question I would have asked: "How long will that take?" His counselor smiled and said, "I would plan on six months." Steve was stunned. Actually, as he described the exchange to me later, he was mad. His words: "I got so mad I pretty much confirmed my need for more counseling." Their counselor recognized that Steve and Shawna wouldn't be grappling with typical first-year marriage problems. They were about to hit the buzz saw of Steve's preexisting condition.

Fortunately for Shawna, Steve did what very few men are willing to do. Two weeks after they returned from their honeymoon, he was back in the counselor's office.

Alone. Why? It certainly wasn't standard operating procedure. Very few people continue counseling *after* their wedding. Heck, most couples don't get counseling *before* their wedding! In light of Steve's past experience, it was the wise thing to do. He's convinced it saved his marriage.

Chances are, there are places you have no business visiting because of your history—places that would have no impact on the average person, but the average person doesn't share your experience with those environments. Perhaps there are types of people you have no business spending time with. Being around them triggers something unhealthy in you. I know people who refuse to use credit cards because of their financial history. Anything inherently wrong with credit cards? Not for most people. But it's unwise for some people.

What about you?

In light of *your* past experience, what is the wise thing for *you* to do? What's the wise thing for you to do financially? Professionally? Relationally? What about your entertainment choices? Where are you set up to fail because of something in your past? Perhaps it's something over which you had no control. Perhaps the way you were raised predisposes you to an arena of temptation to which most people seem immune. If so, admit it. Again, Paul's words: *"Understand what God's will is for you."* Face up to what you know is right for you.

Don't be content with doing the *right* thing. *Do the wise thing.*

So the first of our three reference points is anchored to your past. The second one intersects with your current circumstances.

> *In light of my current circumstances, what is the wise thing for me to do?*

YOUR CURRENT CIRCUMSTANCES

Life is seasonal.

Today's sorrow will be replaced by tomorrow's joy. Today's anger will probably be tempered with tomorrow's perspective. Today's worry will be replaced by tomorrow's concerns. Jesus was correct. Each day has its own worries. If we're not careful, we will allow the pressure, fears, and circumstances of today drive us to make decisions we will regret tomorrow.

That being the case, you owe it to yourself and to the people you love to take your current emotions, state of mind, and perspective into account when making decisions. I don't know about you, but most of my apologies stem from my propensity to react to the moment. When the moment has passed, I discover I've overreacted and hurt someone in the process. I can't begin to remember all the emails I wish I could unsend. If I'd waited twenty-four hours, my response and tone would have been different. There would have been far less residual damage. When I'm mad, the wise thing for me to do is NOTHING. Just wait. Besides, when I'm mad, there's usually something I don't know.

So when asking our fourth question, we would do well to take into account what's going on in the present. In light of our current circumstances and state of mind, what is the wise thing to do? In many instances, the answer is nothing! Wait. Defer. Pause. Postpone. Sit one out.

We have several thousand singles in our Atlanta-area churches. Many are nursing wounds from a divorce. At the same time, they desire companionship. More often than not, before the ink is dry on the divorce papers, they are already moving toward or looking for a new relationship. I imagine I would be tempted to do the same thing.

Obviously, there's nothing wrong with companionship. There's nothing wrong with moving on with our lives once we've closed the door on a difficult chapter. But how and how quickly we move on is important. For single men and women who find themselves in this challenging season, this is the question I encourage them to ask, "In light of what I've just come through . . . in light of my current state of mind, my emotional state, my unresolved anger and hurt . . . what is the wise thing for me to do?"

The answer is never, *Jump into a new relationship as quickly as possible.*

Not because that would be wrong. Because it would be unwise. More often than not, that one unwise relational decision paves the way to a regretful decision. Remember, our greatest regrets are always preceded by a series of unwise decisions. Jumping back into the dating game on the heels of a divorce or breakup is almost always a gateway decision. It leads to regret.

I recognize there's no one-size-fits-all advice for men and women navigating the aftermath of divorce. But my general counsel for years has been to mark their calendars one year from the day their divorce was legal . . . not the day they split with their ex . . . the day their divorce was legal. Men roll their eyes. Women are often quick to assure me the last thing they want in their lives is another man. In both instances, I insist they pull out their phones and mark the date.

Not because it's the right thing to do.

Because it's *the wise thing to do.*

I've never had anyone come back to me and complain about taking a year off from dating. Especially after a divorce or a painful breakup. But through the years, there have been dozens of men and women who've confided in me that they wish they had. I feel so strongly about this that I have asked our pastors not to perform second marriages for individuals who have been divorced for less then two years. Do I have a Bible verse to support this policy? Nope. Is it wrong to remarry before two years have passed? Nope. Then why such a stringent policy?

You already know the answer.

It's the wise thing to do.

I've never heard anyone attribute their marriage problems to the fact that they waited too long to marry. But I've talked to countless folks who wish they had waited longer, especially when there's a divorce in the rearview mirror.

I have no way of knowing if you are wrestling with a decision right now. But while I have your attention, I might as well ask. In light of what's going on in your life right now . . . in light of your recent past, your current state of mind, your physical health, your financial challenges and responsibilities, what is the wise thing for you to do?

YOUR FUTURE HOPES AND DREAMS

Every year or so, I ask the folks in our organization the following question:

What breaks your heart?

This can be a dangerous and dangerously expensive question to answer honestly.

It's led people to quit their jobs to pursue opportunities more in line with their passion and concerns. It's led folks to start nonprofits. Adopt. Foster. Move. Run for office. Go back into teaching. Finish their education.

What breaks my heart is watching people make decisions that undermine their hopes and dreams. It breaks my heart to watch individuals or couples make relationship decisions that will undermine their relationship—current and future. It breaks my heart to watch teenagers make decisions that will result in consequences that follow them around for a decade or two. It breaks my heart to watch parents parent in a way that will eventually drive a wedge between their children and them.

Bottom line, it breaks my heart to watch people engineer their own unhappiness.

This probably explains why I'm convinced this third application of our fourth question is the most important application.

In light of your future hopes and dreams,
what is the wise thing for you to do?

You have some idea of what you want your future to look like. You have a mental picture of your preferred future—what could be and should be—how you envision the next season or two to play out. It may be general. It may be specific. You may have gone to the trouble of writing it down.

Regardless of how much time and effort you've put into it, you have some idea of what you want the future to look like. You may not have a plan for getting there, but you have a general sense of where *there* is. And I'm guessing that when you envision your future, you don't envision yourself alone.

Nobody does.

But here's the challenge.

DREAM WRECKERS

When it comes to our dreams, the deck is stacked against us. There are too many variables, variables we have no control over. Life is hard. And life is particularly hard on our dreams—our preferred future. It's an uphill climb. That being the case, why would we contribute to the demise of what we hope for? Why would anyone rob themselves of their own future? I don't have a good answer to that question.

But it happens all the time.

Right?

You've watched it happen. You've watched friends undermine their financial dreams. You've watched a friend or family member sabotage a relationship through alcohol abuse. You probably know someone whose dishonesty cost them a career. We all know someone whose infidelity cost them their marriage and the respect of their children. Perhaps one of those stories is your story. At some point, we've all done something that jeopardized our hopes and dreams.

Let's not do that anymore.

Let's make today's decisions with tomorrow in mind.

In light of your future hopes and dreams, what is the wise thing for *you* to do?

FUTURE TENSE, COMMON SENSE

Asking our fourth question with the future in mind casts a trenchant light on the legitimacy of our options. The deceptive shades of gray dissipate. Our best option or options become clear. Painfully clear. So clear we are tempted to look away, to retreat to the excuses with which we've buttressed our less-than-wise decisions for years:

I'm not doing anything wrong.

People do this all the time.

I'm not hurting anyone.

I can handle it.

There's no law against it.

God will forgive me.

Our excuses are persuasive because they're mostly true. You aren't doing anything *wrong*. It is *commonplace*. You can handle it, initially. It isn't illegal. God will forgive you.

But so what?

That's all beside the point, right?

The purpose of our fourth question isn't to stop you from doing something *wrong*. It's to keep you from doing something *unwise*. Unwise is the gateway to regret. It paves the way to the tipping point—the point of no return. Anna Nalick nailed it when she penned these lyrics:[3]

> Life's like an hourglass, glued to the table
> No one can find the rewind button girl . . .

Wisdom reduces the likelihood that you'll need a rewind button.

So let's put away our old worn-out excuses once and for all, shall we? They've never served you well. The only

---

3. Anna Nalick, "Breathe (2 AM)," Concord Music Co., copyright 2004.

purpose they've served is to silence your conscience, cloud your reasoning, and diminish your ability to hear the voices of wisdom around you. Your excuses have escorted you to the threshold of regret over and over. They've left you with secrets that you hope the people you care most about never discover. They've left you with stories you'll never share. They've introduced you to shame, memories you can't erase, and seasons you can't forget. Your excuses have facilitated the demise of your hopes and dreams. They are not your friends.

So decide . . .

Decision #4: The Maturity Decision
I will do the *wise* thing.

LET'S GET SPECIFIC

In light of where you want to be financially in ten years, what's the wise thing to do now? What do you need to start or stop doing financially? What habit or habits do you need to break? If you've given *little to no thought* about where you want to be financially ten years from now, that's part of the problem. Set three high-level, general goals. Put 'em somewhere you can look at them every day. They will inform your conscience and serve as guardrails to your spending and use of debt. Most importantly, they will serve as context for all your financial decisions. Face it, you are going to be somewhere financially five or ten years from now. Shouldn't *you* decide? If you don't decide, retailers and lenders who care nothing about you will decide for you.

What is true for your financial future is also true for your relational, professional, and academic future. Where do you want to be? Decide. Write it down. If you're single, in light of what you ultimately want relationally . . . romantically . . . what is the wisest way to conduct your relationships now? What are you doing now that has the potential to rob you of your preferred future relationally? What can you do to set yourself up for success later? Decide and live accordingly.

If you're married and plan to go the distance with your spouse, finish together . . . enjoy grandchildren together, what can you do now to facilitate that dream? What puts that dream at risk? What precautions need to be taken? What's the wise thing to do as it relates to protecting your marriage?

Got kids?

What do you envision for your relationship with your children when they're teenagers or in college or married with children of their own? What is the wise thing to do now to protect that dream? What practices would you be wise to incorporate now into your parenting repertoire? Where do you need to reprioritize? What do you need to say no to? Not because it's wrong or bad, but because it's interfering with where you want to be? When our three children were young, Sandra and I adopted a mantra:

No for now, but not forever.

We eliminated several categories of activities from our calendar until our children were in middle school. We said no to things during that season that we would say yes to once they were older. Our goal as parents was simple. If you have kids at home, I recommend you consider borrowing it. Our goal was for our children to *want* to be together and to *want* to be with us when they no longer had to be.

We established that goal when our oldest was still in a car seat. All three of our kids are in their mid to late twenties. They love to be together. They enjoy being with us. We said no to some good things so we could eventually enjoy the best things. Speaking from personal experience, whatever you have to give up now to get there later is worth it. And the same is true in every arena of life.

But . . .

But if you never stop long enough to *decide* ahead of time where you want to be, you will live your life unaware of the sacrifices necessary to get there.

Everybody ends up somewhere in life. I recommend you end up somewhere on purpose.

Wisdom paves the way.

PUTTING IT ALL TOGETHER

When sharing our fourth question with high school and college students, I encourage them to commit the following rhyme to memory:

There's good and there's bad, but that's not my Q,
but rather, What is the wise thing to do?

Don't settle for good, legal, permissible, acceptable, tolerable, not prosecutable, or normal. If you do, you will eventually find yourself living dangerously close to regret. You're better than that. You deserve better than that. Your family deserves better than that.

If you had been asking this catalytic question all along, you might have avoided your greatest regret. More importantly, if you begin asking this question now, you significantly decrease the chances of that bit of unfortunate history repeating itself.

So, resist the temptation to hide behind broad generalities and cultural norms. What is the wise thing for *you* to do? You are a unique blend of past experiences, current circumstances, and future hopes and dreams. Wisdom allows you to customize the decision-making process to your specific professional, financial, and relational aspirations. Don't miss this opportunity.

Imagine how different your life would be now if you had been processing your options this way from the beginning. Imagine how different your life might look a year from now if this multifaceted question was part of your decision-making grid from this point forward.

So, ask it.

Ask it even if you don't plan to act on it. You owe it to yourself to know. You owe it to the people depending on you as well.

So, one last time:

In light of your past experience,
your current circumstances,
and your future hopes and dreams,
what is the wise thing to do?

— 6 —

The Relationship
Question

What Does Love Require of Me?

By now it should be unsettlingly clear that the very thing that makes our questions clarifying has the potential to make them a bit terrifying as well. I'm referring to the fact that we usually know the answers before we finish asking the questions. And once we know, we can't unknow. And once we know, we feel accountable.

It's terrible.

It reminds me of a question my mentor Regi Campbell used to ask:

"Andy, what do you hope I don't ask you about?"

To which I would reply,

"That's cheating! You're supposed to poke around and discover that for yourself!"

He would laugh and then repeat the question, "So, what do you hope I don't ask you about?"

I still made him dig.

Our final question may be the most clarifying and terrifying of all. But clarity is often the very thing we need to push us past our resistance. And there *will* be resistance with this one. This will be the question you will be most tempted not to answer honestly. So, once again, the disclaimer: You don't have to *do* anything with your answer. But you owe it to yourself to know . . . admit . . . acknowledge . . . the answer. What you *won't* know can hurt you. What you refuse to acknowledge will follow you into your future. It will shape the story of your life. In the case of our final question, what you don't or won't know has the potential to hurt you where you have the potential to hurt most . . . in your most cherished relationships.

As the chapter title indicates, this is the relationship question.

We've never met. I know I keep saying that.

We've never met, but here's what I know about you. You do not envision your future alone. There's somebody beside you. Perhaps that somebody is already beside you. Our final question will help you keep them there. Perhaps you're looking for that somebody. This question will equip you to choose the right somebody. But the benefit of this question extends beyond that special somebody. This question, when asked and answered, has the potential to enhance the quality of every relationship. It has the power to restore and heal broken relationships. It has the power to rekindle romance. It has the potential to restore what was lost.

One more disclaimer.

It may not work.

Our first four questions come with a guaranteed ROI (Return on investment). You'll always come out ahead by discovering *why* you're doing what you're doing . . . really. You'll have something to show for writing a story you want to tell. There will be a positive, often measurable return for paying attention to the tension and doing the wise thing. These four questions always yield a favorable return. Often immediately. Always eventually. Either way, they will pay. Asking and answering honestly will make your life better.

Our fifth and final question is different.

There may be no tangible, measurable, or even noticeable return on your effort with this one. While the first four questions are demanding in the moment, our final question is demanding throughout every waking moment of every day. The reason being, our final question isn't about making *your* life better. It's about making *someone else's* life better, which may make your life better. But it may not.

So why bother?

Glad you asked.

Our final question, should you have the courage to ask and act on it, positions you to make the *world* better.

Here we go.

THE OTHER RULE

No doubt you're familiar with the Golden Rule. Multiple versions can be found in both religious and nonreligious literature dating back to the time of Confucius.[1] Every major world religion includes some form of the famous equation. Matthew's Gospel records Jesus's version:

> So in everything, do to others what you would have them do to you, for this sums up the Law and the Prophets.[2]

According to Jesus, this simple, universal maxim "sums up" the six-hundred-plus laws included in the ancient Hebrew law code. If you've read or attempted to read the ancient Hebrew law code as presented in Leviticus, Numbers, or Deuteronomy, you know that's saying a lot.

While the Golden Rule is good advice to be sure, it has its limitations. Even this seemingly unassailable, universally accepted maxim falls short of our fifth and final question. But before you accuse me of attempting to improve on the words of Jesus (or Confucius), you should know it was Jesus himself who raised the bar and upped the ante.

Here's what happened.

SOMETHING NEW

Throughout Jesus's ministry, he hinted that something new was on the horizon, something designed to replace much of what was in place in first-century Palestine. While many hoped for political reform, Jesus had something different

---

1. 551–479 BC.
2. Matthew 7:12.

in mind. Something bigger. More inclusive. Something that would extend beyond his earthly ministry. On one occasion he predicted a new movement or assembly.[3] On several occasions he claimed to be the end or fulfillment of the current religious establishment.[4] He claimed to be greater than the temple. A claim that, if true, would make the temple and all it represented obsolete.[5] To punctuate that point, he claimed the ability to forgive sin, thus negating the need for the arduous sacrificial system associated with the temple.[6]

All his hints, allusions, and insinuations were designed to create a sense of expectation in the minds and hearts of his followers. In that he was successful. When he entered Jerusalem for his final visit, crowds lined the streets to welcome him. Their expectations were political, regal, messianic. He had their attention, but they did not understand his intentions. Even his twelve apostles were confused regarding his ultimate aim. Right up to the end, they were jockeying for positions of power in the soon-to-be-revitalized kingdom of Israel. So on the night of his arrest, he made his intentions clear.

Frighteningly clear.

To begin with, he announced he was leaving.

My children, I will be with you only a little longer . . .
Where I am going, you cannot come.[7]

---

3. See Matthew 16:18.
4. See Matthew 5:17.
5. See Matthew 12:6 and Hebrews 8:7, 13.
6. See Mark 2:5.
7. John 13:33.

Several in the room, Peter in particular, didn't hear anything after that. Jesus was their security blanket. Wherever Jesus went, crowds gathered and Jesus's enemies weren't welcome. If Jesus went missing, odds were they would go missing as well. And not in a good way. Besides, why would he leave now? They were on the precipice of a revolution. The kingdom of Israel was about to be restored.

Jesus continued.

A new command I give you . . .[8]

A new command? They didn't need any new commands. The six-hundred-plus they had kept 'em plenty busy. Besides, earlier, Jesus had reduced their entire list to two: love God and love your neighbor.[9] So why add a third? And why was he even talking about commands? They needed to make plans. Besides, *what gave Jesus the right to add any new commands?* Grouping and prioritizing commandments was one thing. Adding to them? Only God had the authority to do that.

Then again, only God had the authority to forgive sin.

As it turned out, Jesus wasn't adding a command to an existing list of commands. He was doing something far more radical. He was replacing the existing ones. He continued:

A new command I give you, love one another . . .

---

8. John 13:34.
9. Matthew 22:38–39.

Clearly Jesus wasn't commanding them to *feel* something. He was commanding them to *do* something. But loving *one another* wasn't really new. As it turns out, Jesus wasn't really through. What came next was, well, unthinkable. But what came next changed the world.

What Jesus said next is the basis for our fifth and final question.

What came next trumped the Golden Rule. I call it the platinum rule.

As *I* have loved you, so you must love one another.[10]

That was new.

That was blasphemous.

There was no getting around it. Jesus claimed to be the gold or platinum standard for love. Apparently, doing for others what one hoped others would do in return was so . . . so last century. Jesus instructed his followers to do unto one another as *he* had done unto them. This was extraordinarily personal for the men seated around that table. When Christians read, "As I have loved you," we think of the cross.

They didn't.

They thought back over the previous three years. Perhaps each man in the room was transported back to a particular moment in time when Jesus had *loved* them particularly well. He could have called 'em out one by one.

---

10. John 13:34.

"Matthew, remember what you were up to the first time we met?"

"Yes, sir. I was working for Rome from home. I was . . . well, I was a thief. Good people kept their distance."

"Remember what I said to you that afternoon?"

"Yes, sir. You invited me to follow you. Nobody had ever done that before. Well . . . nobody of repute."

"Exactly. Matthew, extend that same grace to everyone you meet for the rest of your life. As I have loved you . . ."

He could have worked his way around the table. One by one. Love as I have loved you.

Extend the same grace and forgiveness I extended to you to everybody you meet. And he could have added: "And gentlemen, if you think you've seen me love . . . tighten your sandals . . . you ain't seen nothing yet." Little did they know that on the following day, he would put on a demonstration of love that would take their breath away. He would give his life away.

Jesus continued,

> By *this* everyone will know that you are my disciples, if you love one another.[11]

The term *this* is a demonstrative pronoun. Remember those? Demonstrative pronouns are used to point to something specific. In this particular case, it's a *singular*

---

11. John 13:35.

demonstrative pronoun. Jesus pointed to one specific thing that was to be *the* identifying characteristic of his followers—the way they loved. This new-command brand was to serve as the unifying and defining characteristic for his new movement. His *ekklesia*. His new command was to serve as the governing ethic, the standard against which all behavior was to be measured for those who called him Lord.

His primary concern was not that they *believe* something. He insisted they *do* something. They were to love as he had loved. The men gathered that night had an inkling as to what that might look like. In a few hours, it would become astonishingly clear.

WHERE ANGELS FEAR

Jesus's new command involved another subtle-but-striking shift in the world order. Jesus didn't tether his new command to the anchor all religious commands were traditionally tethered: love for, fear of, dedication to God. Jesus tethered his new command to himself. Again, he inserted himself into an equation mere mortals had no business inserting themselves into.

The litmus test for being a bona fide Jesus follower was not the ritualistic, day-of-the-week, festival-driven, don't-forget-your-goat worship of an invisible and somewhat distant God.

Following Jesus would not be about looking for ways to get closer to God who dwelled out there, up there, somewhere. Jesus followers would demonstrate their devotion to God by putting the person next to them in front of them. Authentic Jesus followers wouldn't authenticate their love for God by looking up. They would authenticate their devotion by looking around.

But the shift didn't stop there.

Conspicuously absent from Jesus's new-command instructions was an overt reference to his divine right to require such allegiance and obedience. In what is arguably his most future-defining set of instructions, Jesus refused to play the God card. Even in this final, if-you-forget-everything-else-I've-said exchange, Jesus did not leverage his holiness, his personal righteousness, or even his divinely granted moral authority.

Jesus leveraged his example[12]—how he loved.

Jesus's love *for* the men in the room, rather than his authority *over* the men in the room, is what he leveraged to *instruct* and *inspire* the men in the room. The men in that room would not see him seated on a Jewish throne. They would see him hanging from a Roman cross. It was his gory and gritty sacrifice, not a keep-your-hands-clean holiness, that compelled his disciples to eventually take up their own crosses and follow him.

If you are a Christian, that should stop you in your tracks.

A few years later, it would stop Paul in his:

12. See John 13:15.

In your *relationships* with *one another*, have the same mindset as Christ Jesus: Who, being in very nature God, did not consider equality with God something to be *used to his own advantage*;

Jesus never played the God card.

. . . rather, he made himself *nothing* by taking the very nature of a servant, being made in human likeness. And being found in appearance as a man, he humbled himself by becoming obedient to death—

But not just any death—a death no mere mortal would willingly subject themselves to.

∴ . . . even death on a cross![13]

Jesus did not leverage his equality with God to stir his followers to action.

He leveraged his love.

Jesus didn't anchor his new command to his divine right as king. He anchored it to his sacrificial love. Why should his disciples obey his command to love? Because he loved them first. He loved them best. They were to do unto others as Jesus had already done . . . and was about to do . . . unto them. Hours later, Jesus staged a demonstration of love that not only took their breath away, it took their excuses away as well, along with ours. Jesus leveraged selfless love to compel his followers to love.

---

13. Philippians 2:5–8, emphasis added.

By *this* everyone will know that you are my disciples,
if you love one another.[14]

Jesus's new, all-encompassing command was far *less*
complicated than the prevailing system. But it was far *more*
demanding. There are no loopholes, no work-arounds in
this brand of love.

GROUND RULES

Sandra and I are foster parents. Through the years we've
had a dozen or so kids in and out of our home. Always
sibling groups. Our forever foster daughter came to live
with us the first time when she was ten. She and her two
sisters lived with us for four months before moving in
with another foster family who was pursuing adoption.
Long story short, her sisters were eventually adopted by
that family, but Sierra opted out of the adoption process
and went to live in a group home.[15] After another short
stint with a second foster family, she landed in a second
group home. That's when we stepped back into her life and
brought her home to live with us full-time. By this time,
Sierra was fifteen.

There's generally a honeymoon period with foster kids.
Since Sierra had been in our home off and on for over five
years, our honeymoon was short. I remember the afternoon
it ended. Sierra came downstairs with a darker than usual

---

14. John 13:35.
15. Sierra is a fictional name.

look on her face, sat down at the kitchen counter, and said, "Okay, so what are the rules?"

We'd known Sierra long enough to know that she wasn't asking in order to ensure she didn't accidentally break our rules. She was asking so she could figure out how to get *around* our rules. This was her MO, and it may have contributed to the fact that we were her third foster family. Just sayin'.

I smiled and said, "Sierra, you've been around our family enough to know that's not how we operate. We don't have a list of rules." And we didn't. Never did. Still don't. When our three kids were young, we had two rules: Honor your mother and don't tell a lie. I didn't require our kids to honor me. If they honored Sandra, that was enough. Honoring someone important to me was all the honor I needed. When they didn't honor their mother, they had to deal with me.

When it came to telling the truth, my mantra was, "Kids, the worst thing you can do is tell a lie . . . because lying breaks a relationship. And I don't want our relationship to break."

Anyway.

Sierra wanted an answer, so I asked her to sit tight while I went back to my home office, pulled out a 3×5 card, wrote a single word on it, and took it back to the kitchen. I slid it across the counter and said, "This is how we do it here." The card read: HONOR.

She rolled her eyes, pushed her stool back from the counter, and went upstairs to her room. She never touched the card. I left it on the counter for several days. I still have it. And I would love to report that my insightful and oh-so-creative response revolutionized Sierra's life.

It didn't.

It didn't make a dent.

She wanted rules. She wanted rules because she wanted control. Give me five rules and I'll find a loophole. Give me ten rules and I'll find even more loopholes. When I'm discussing this principle with pastors, I often say, "Give me the entire Bible and I'll find you justification for just about any behavior you need justification for." It usually gets real quiet at that point. They understand exactly what I'm saying.

Rules create wiggle room. You were sixteen once. You remember.

"You said to be home by 9:00. You didn't say 9:00 p.m."

But that kind of thinking doesn't end with frontal lobe development.

"The company handbook doesn't mention that specifically, so it must be okay."

"Technically, I didn't . . ."

"There's no law against . . ."

"All I said was . . ."

Sierra is twenty-one now. She gave me permission to tell our story. Our honor culture did little to curb her quest to do things her way. But it certainly created the foundation for the relationship we have with her today. Relationships are built on mutual honor and respect, not rules.

And that brings us at last to our final question. The relationship question. The question that paves the path to relational health but doesn't guarantee the other person will choose to walk it with you—the question that lays a foundation for mutually beneficial relationships but comes with no promise the other party will choose to build on it. It's a question that introduces inescapable clarity to just about every moral, ethical, and relational decision you will bump up against. Our final question takes us to the heart of Jesus's new covenant command—the standard by which his followers are required to evaluate their behavior, conversations, and attitudes—a question I'm quick to invite even religious skeptics to adopt because of its relationally healing properties and potential.

Question #5: The Relationship Question
What does love *require* of me?

This clarifying, but terrifying question should stand guard over our consciences. It should serve as guide, signpost, and compass as we navigate the unavoidable complexities inherent in every relationship. It should inform how we date, parent, boss, manage, and coach. It should form a perimeter around what we say and do in our roles as spouses, coworkers, and neighbors.

This question gives voice to God's will for us on issues where the Bible, as well as all other religious literature, is silent. It fills the gaps with disquieting precision. It succeeds where concordances fail. It quashes the insipid justification,

"But the Bible doesn't say there's anything wrong with
_____." It closes loopholes. It exposes hypocrisy. It stands
as judge and jury. It's so simple. But it's so inescapably
demanding.

Our final question, fueled and informed by Jesus's "as I
have loved you" *command*, intersects with every imaginable
relational scenario. We are all tempted at times to ask or
wonder how little we can get by with relationally . . . the
very thing we don't want the person on the other side of
us to consider. This question calls us to account. When
presenting this concept publically, I often ask the audience
to commit the following to memory:

> When unsure of what to say or do,
> ask what love requires of you.

We don't need chapter and verse. We have something better.
Namely, Jesus's new, all-encompassing, inescapably simple
command. We are to do unto others as our heavenly Father,
through Christ, has done unto us. He did what was best for
us. We, in turn, are to do what's best for others even when
less than what's best is embraced as acceptable by the others.

I would imagine you are smart enough and emotionally
dialed in enough to know what love requires of you 90
percent of the time. When it comes to the other 10 percent,
there's probably a handful of folks around that would be
willing to help you sort through your options. If you have
middle school or high school students in your home, it may
feel more like 70/30 or 60/40. Parenting is . . . well . . . it's

not for the faint of heart. Either way, we almost always know what love requires.

But just in case . . .

DEFINING TERMS

If *love* is not specific enough, worry not. The instructions and directives scattered throughout the New Testament serve as real-world applications of what Jesus's new-command brand of love looks like. These New Testament imperatives clarify what's required of those who have the courage to ask. The authors of the New Testament did not add to Jesus's "new command." They simply applied it for their readers. And for us.

The apostle Paul provides us with the clearest applications. In his letter to Christians living in the Roman province of Galatia, he insists that when it comes to relationships, God will always nudge us in the direction of kindness, goodness, gentleness, faithfulness, and self-control.[16]

When in doubt, max those out.

But that's the abridged list.

WHAT LOVE REQUIRES

Paul's most detailed description of what real-world love looks and acts like is found in his first letter to Christians living in first-century Corinth. This particular passage is so

---

16. Galatians 5:22.

familiar, I fear it doesn't create so much as a ripple in the consciences of most modern readers. We've relegated these words to weddings and love songs. That's unfortunate. Paul's compelling and clarifying description of what love looks like and acts like is the gold standard. Because so many of us are so familiar with Paul's words, I've chosen to present them as an answer to our question: What does love require of us?[17]

Here we go.

Love requires patience.[18] Love is not pushy. Love requires that I move at your pace rather than requiring you to move at mine.

Love requires kindness.[19] Kindness is love's response to weakness. Kindness is the choice to loan others our strength rather than reminding them of their weaknesses. It's doing for others what they cannot in that moment do for themselves.

Love requires us to keep envy and pride from interfering with our ability to celebrate the success of others.[20] Love requires us to allow others to shine. It isn't threatened by the success of others.

Love requires us to show honor to others. Love never treats another person dishonorably, disgracefully, or indecently.[21] Love doesn't create regret. After all, honor is at the heart of every satisfying relationship.

---

17. The following is adapted from the New Testament book of 1 Corinthains, chapter 13.

18. 1 Corinthians 13:4.

19. 1 Corinthians 13:4.

20. See 1 Corinthians 13:4.

21. 1 Corinthians 13:5.

Love requires selflessness. Love is not self-seeking or selfish.[22] It puts the interests and needs of others first. That alone would solve most relationship problems.

Love requires us to address our anger privately rather than allowing it to spill out on the people around us. Love requires us to own it and goes to work on it. Paul says, love is "not easily angered."[23] It's not easily stirred up or provoked. Instead, love absorbs. Love puts the other person's story ahead of our own.

Love requires us to forgive. Love "keeps no record of wrongs."[24] Funny thing about relational record keepers. They rarely keep track of their own records. Do you enjoy catching your spouse or significant other messing up? That's messed up. Forgiving and pretending to forget is your best bet. That's what love requires. To do otherwise is a power play. When someone holds your past over you, who's in the elevated position? Love is not about powering up. Love is about stepping down.

Paul's final descriptors are best taken together as one big game-changing idea.

Love does not delight in evil but rejoices with the truth. It always protects . . . always trusts, always hopes, always perseveres.[25]

---

22. 1 Corinthians 13:5.
23. 1 Corinthians 13:5.
24. 1 Corinthians 13:5.
25. 1 Corinthians 13:6–7).

Love requires us to see and believe the best while choosing to downplay the rest. We might as well believe the best about each other. Nothing is gained by doing otherwise. Love chooses a *generous explanation* when others don't meet our expectations.

Paul says love "always protects." Love requires us to do everything in our power to *protect* or guard the relationship. Translated: Love doesn't smuggle harmful things into a relationship. Just the opposite. Love keeps harmful things out.

That's quite a list.

But that's what love requires.

That's why our fifth question is not for the faint of heart.

But before you go looking for a Sharpie to scratch out *Five questions to . . .* and substitute *Four questions . . .* instead, consider this. Aren't the adjectives and verbs in Paul's list the very things you hope for or even expect from the people closest to you? Your spouse, fiancé, significant other, kids? Isn't this what you hope for from your friends, neighbors, and coworkers? In some respect, you expect the people you love most to exhibit some form of everything referenced above. If these are the behaviors and responses we consciously or subconsciously expect or hope for from others . . . shouldn't they be required of us as well?

It goes without saying, but I'll say it anyway: when two people or two parties embrace this approach, amazing things happen. There's virtually no obstacle that can't be overcome. If that sounds like hyperbole, think back to your last relational conflict at work. What if you and your supervisor, partner, associate, or employee had both approached the conversation having predecided to protect the relationship and not to dishonor the other party. Different tone? Different outcome? Probably.

Think back to your most recent conflict with a family member or significant other. Would the tone and temperature of that conversation have been different if both parties had predecided not to be *self-seeking* and to *protect* the relationship at all costs? Predeciding to *protect* the integrity of a relationship redefines what it means to win. Love doesn't seek to win the argument. Love seeks to protect the relationship. Besides, nobody ever *wins* an argument when family is involved. I've seen too many parents *win* all the arguments and *lose* their kids in the process.

So, what does love require of you?

It may require you to close this book, get up out of your chair, walk into the kitchen or bedroom, and apologize.

I'll wait.

It may require you to pick up your phone and rebuild a bridge you burned with your unassailable logic and sarcasm. You were right! But being *right* wasn't what love required of you. You may need to write a letter. Rewrite an email. Invite someone to meet you for coffee. And *no*, the other party may not be interested in what love requires of you. They may have no interest in what love requires of *them* either.

I warned you.

There's no guaranteed return on investment with this question.

But this is how we make the world better. And, if we're honest, this is how we want to be treated by others. So, here's our fifth and final decision . . . should you choose to decide it.

Decision #5: The Relationship Decision
I will decide with the interests of others in mind.

NOT ALWAYS CLEAR

I'm not always sure what to believe. My views on a variety of topics have morphed, evolved, or completely changed through the years. This includes my views on parenting, politics, marriage, leadership, and money, just to name a few. One of the humbling things about being a pastor is that my views on just about everything are documented somewhere on a hard drive. Every preacher I know wishes they could go back and repreach, unpreach, or delete some old messages. We meant well. But then life happened. Kids happened. Tragedy struck. We grew. We matured. We saw the world differently. The world didn't change. We did.

If you're honest, you're not always sure what to believe either. But be encouraged. Even the apostle Paul, with all his mind-bending insight, wisdom, and experience, was in the same boat. At the end of his challenging description of what love requires, he concluded with the following:

For we know in *part* and we prophesy in *part*, but when *completeness* comes, what is in part disappears . . .[26]

 For now we see only a reflection as in a mirror; then we shall see face to face. Now I know in *part*; then I shall know *fully*, even as I am fully known.[27]

Like us, Paul had questions. He only knew "in part." There were things even he couldn't sort out, questions he didn't have answers for. This was from the man who provided us with half the New Testament. If Paul only knew in part, what do I know? What do you know? On our best days, we know "in part." But the part that makes his admission so fascinating is the context. They are sandwiched between the following lines:

Love never fails. But where there are prophecies, they will cease; where there are tongues, they will be stilled; where there is knowledge, it will pass away.[28]

 And now these three remain: faith, hope and love. But the greatest of these is love.[29]

His meaning is plain.
We know what we know, but we don't know everything.
We see what we see, but we can't see everything.

---

26. 1 Corinthians 13:9.
27. 1 Corinthians 13:12, emphasis added.
28. 1 Corinthians 13:8.
29. 1 Corinthians 13:13.

Once we've learned all we can learn, there will still be more to learn.

We believe what we believe, but our beliefs are limited by what we know, see, and experience. Yet while our knowledge and beliefs are in flux, one thing is not. There is one thing that transcends our limited knowledge, insight, and experience.

Love.

Love fills the gaps. Love reduces the friction created by our limited insight, knowledge, and judgment-inhibiting experiences. There is much I don't know. There are things I'll never understand. But my ignorance does not impede my capacity to put others first.

So while I'm not always sure what to believe, and while my views on a variety of things continue to mature and change, I almost always know what *love requires of me*.

I bet you do too.

Conclusion

I began our journey with tales of my father's reluctance to tell me what to do when I didn't know what to do. Ultimately, it made me a better decision-maker and gave me an appreciation for the relationship between *good questions* and *good decisions*. But his investment in my future certainly went beyond asking inconvenient questions. Around the time I turned five or six years old, my dad began encouraging me to do something I continue to do to this day.

He suggested I begin by asking God to show me his will for my life.

So I did.

Every night I would conclude my bedtime prayer routine with ". . . and please show me your will for my life, amen."

Unfortunately, it was during that same season my parents introduced me to that disturbing piece of narrative from the Old Testament when God speaks audibly to a fourth grader in the middle of the night.

Familiar with that?

Actually, we don't know what grade Samuel was in when this occurred. But we know he was young. If you're not familiar with the story: Samuel's mom, Hannah, had trouble getting pregnant. She and her husband Elkanah had tried for years but to no avail. Adding insult to injury, Elkanah had two wives. Peninnah, wife number two, had no trouble whatsover getting pregnant. So Hannah was greatly distressed. In her desperation, she vowed to God that if he would give her a son, she would give him back to serve in whatever manner God chose. God granted her request, and she named her son Samuel. And true to her vow, she took him to the prophet Eli and left him there to serve alongside the aging prophet.

So far so good.

Then, one night, young Samuel hears a voice calling his name. He assumes it's Eli, so he runs to Eli's bedside. Turns out it wasn't Eli. This happens two more times. Eli realizes something is up and tells Samuel that if he hears the voice again to respond: "Speak LORD, for your servant is listening."[1] Sure enough, it was the voice of God. And God gives him a glimpse into the future.

The moral of the story, according to my parents anyway, was to be listening on the off chance God chose to speak to me the way he did to little Samuel. And if so, I was to respond as Samuel did.

However.

I'm confident if God . . . or anyone for that matter . . .

---

1. 1 Samuel 3:9.

whispered my name in the middle of the night, my parents would have had to change my sheets in the middle of the same night. Theirs as well. I would have most certainly spent the rest of the night sandwiched between the pair of them.

Now, you're going to think I'm making this next part up, but I'm not. I was so disturbed by the notion of God speaking to me in the dark that I actually added an addendum to my prayers. ". . . but not tonight. Please show me your will in the daytime."

No lie.

During high school, I often wondered if I'd missed God's will. I wasn't always paying attention in that particular season. Truth be told, there were occasions when I hoped God was busy showing somebody else his will for their life. I had a pretty good idea of what I wanted to do with mine. And I was confident our wills didn't line up.

But in spite of my childhood misgivings and teenage misbehaving, I continued to ask God to show me his will. Over time, my ask was more targeted. I began asking God to show me his will regarding friends, girlfriends, jobs, college major, summer opportunities. Pretty much everything. And I'm glad I did. This simple habit kept me looking up and looking ahead. It provided me with a sense of destiny. If God had a will or plan for my life, I certainly didn't want to miss it. If God had a plan for my life, what could possibly be more important?

So when my kids were old enough to begin developing a faith of their own, I encouraged them to ask God to show them his will for their lives. And just like me, they tacked it on to the end of their nightly prayers: ". . . and please show me your will for my life, amen."

But I did not use the story of Samuel as a selling point.

A WILL FOR YOUR LIFE

There has always been a debate among people of faith as to whether God has a specific plan for each individual. A case can be made for both sides of that debate. But at sixty-two, I'm still asking God to show me his will.

You'd think I'd know by now, right?

So why ask?

Same reasons I've always asked. It keeps me looking up and looking ahead. It continues to provide me with a sense of destiny. Besides, new chapters come with new opportunities and challenges that require new insight and understanding. Every season of life has left me more dependent and more in need of grace and direction. My experience has confirmed what I only suspected as a teenager: *Nothing is more fulfilling.* There is no peace like the peace that comes with knowing you are in sync with God's will for your life.

In case you're wondering, I have yet to hear a voice in the middle of the night. I've never heard a voice in the middle of the day either. Something in me still prefers not to!

And what, you may be wondering, does any of this have to do with our five questions?

In hindsight . . . everything.

Our five questions are more than a decision-making filter. These questions will steer you in the direction of God's *general* will for your life. And . . . and this is big . . . they will position you to discern or recognize his *personal* will for your life as well.

Generally speaking, it is God's will that everyone be honest with themselves . . . really. It's God's will that we all pay attention to anything that dings our consciences. It's God's will for each of us to take into account our past experiences, current circumstances, and future hopes and dreams. It's God's will that we understand what love requires of us. So each of our five questions points us in the direction of God's general will for our lives. His *general* will is directional. In most instances, it's all the direction we need.

When I choose to tell myself the truth even when the truth makes me feel bad about myself, I *see the way* forward. When I choose to explore rather than ignore my conscience, I gain *clarity*. When I pause mid-decision to ask, *What is the wise thing to do*, I usually know before I finish asking the question. When I'm tempted to win an argument at the expense of a relationship and I remember to consider *what love requires* of me, my defenses come down. When I have the presence of mind to consider the story I want to tell, I choose the better story.

But that's not all.

Ordering our lives around these five questions keeps us in a posture of submission. They keep us looking up. A posture of submission positions us to more easily discern

God's *personal will* for our lives. And lest you think I'm making all of this up, the apostle Paul said as much two thousand years ago in his famous letter to Christians living in Rome. He writes:

> I urge you, brothers and sisters, in view of God's mercy, to offer your bodies as a living sacrifice, holy and pleasing to God—this is your true and proper worship.[2]

Translated: Submit yourself to God; it's the logical thing to do. After all, he's God. What follows is the most familiar part and perhaps the most instructive part as well:

> Do not conform to the pattern of this world, but be transformed by the renewing of your mind.[3]

All five of our questions fit neatly in the *renew your mind* bucket. All five stand in sharp contrast to *the pattern of this world*. The pattern of this world is . . . well . . . it's the pattern of the world: Lie to yourself about yourself so you won't feel bad about yourself. Ignore your conscience. Ignore wisdom and snuggle up to disaster. Do what you want to do, not what love requires of you. Write a story that makes you a liar for life; a story you hope you never have to tell.

What Paul writes next serves as the hinge that connects

---

2. Romans 12:1.
3. Romans 12:1.

our five questions with God's *personal* will for our lives. He writes:

> Then . . .

"Then," as in after you renew your mind. But not until then.

> Then you will be able to test and approve what *God's will is*—

That's the connection.

Renewing our minds positions us to discern, figure out, or understand God's *personal* will, his will for *you*. According to Paul, renewing our minds prepares us to hear from God on those occasions when his general will is not enough.

Paul completes his thought with a description of God's will for you:

> Then you will be able to test and approve what *God's will is*—his good, pleasing and *perfect* will.[4]

WRAPPING UP

Good *questions* lead to better *decisions*. Your decisions determine the direction and quality of your life. Your

---

4. Romans 12:2.

decisions serve as the framework for the story of your life. So write a good one. While there's nothing you can do about the decisions you'd choose to go back and unmake, remember this: Your regrets are only *part* of your story. They don't have to be *the* story. Your past should *remind* you. It doesn't have to *define* you.

Begin today incorporating our five questions into the rhythm of your life. Decide to tell yourself the truth even when the truth makes you feel bad about yourself. Explore rather than ignore your conscience. Raise your standard of living from what's acceptable to what's wise. Do what love requires of you. Write a story you are proud to tell—a story distinguished by better decisions, fewer regrets.

Appendix:
The Five Questions

1. The **Integrity** Question
   Am I being honest with myself, really?

   Decision #1: I will not lie to myself even if the truth makes me feel bad about myself.

2. The **Legacy** Question
   What story do I want to tell?

   Decision #2: I will write a story I'm proud to tell one decision at a time.

3. The **Conscience** Question
   Is there a tension that needs my attention?

   Decision #3: I will explore rather than ignore my conscience.

4. The **Maturity** Question
   What is the wise thing to do?

   Decision #4: I will take the past, present, and future into consideration.

5. The **Relationship** Question
   What does love require of me?

   Decision #5: I will decide with the interests of others in mind.

Acknowledgments

No book is the product of individual effort. This book is certainly no exception. The seed for this book was planted years ago by my dad, Dr. Charles Stanley. Growing up, it was his persistent and at times disquieting questions that helped me connect the dots between good questions and good decisions. Thank you, Dad!

On the publishing side, I'm grateful to my friends at Zondervan. John Raymond in particular. Thank you for allowing me to leverage your reputation and reach. A good publisher makes an author better. Zondervan has made me better.

Facilitating the path from an author's ideas to a product someone can hold in their hands is laden with endless details, rabbit trails, and delays. This project would have never gotten off the starting blocks or to the finish line without the relentless focus, time, and energy of Suzy Gray. Suzy, your immediate passion for this content was what launched me on yet another publishing marathon. Your life, your faith, and your story is a constant reminder that a "you" is always more important than a "view." Your life is certainly a story worth telling. Thank you!

New Video Study for Your Church or Small Group

If you've enjoyed this book, now you can go deeper with the companion video Bible study!

In this six-session study, Andy Stanley helps you apply the principles in *Better Decisions, Fewer Regrets* to your life. The study guide includes video notes, group discussion questions, and personal study and reflection materials for in between sessions.

Study Guide	DVD with Free Streaming Access
9780310126560	9780310126584

Available now at your favorite bookstore,
or streaming video on StudyGateway.com.